A GUIDE TO CHORD-MELODY

JAZZ GUITAR

By Toby Wine

ISBN 978-1-5756-0634-7

Visit Hal Leonard Online at
www.halleonard.com

CONTENTS

INTRODUCTION

The world of solo jazz guitar is as vast and limitless as your imagination. Often called "chord melody" playing because of the practice of harmonizing a song's melodies and solos with full chord voicings, this style puts every facet of the guitarist's abilities to the test. Left and right hand techniques, single-line soloing, walking bass lines and grooves, chord playing, and timekeeping are all put into vivid relief without any other instruments to hide behind, and a guitarist's creativity and resourcefulness must come to the fore. Pioneering jazz guitarist George Van Eps (among others) was fond of calling his instrument a "lap piano," and it's an apt description, especially in the solo jazz context. While many guitarists are content playing single-line solos peppered with a few chord forms memorized to provide accompaniment to others, the chord melody player must truly play the entire instrument, top to bottom, single notes to chords to bass lines, often all at once. Within the pages of this book, we'll introduce intermediate and advanced players to the chord melody style, review some of the requisite skills needed to play and create original arrangements, memorize basic chord forms and inversions, examine chord substitution, walking bass lines and other tricks of the trade, and get our feet wet with eight original solo arrangements of some of the most cherished, best-known standards in the jazz repertoire.

The solo jazz guitarist resides in a world of infinite options. The song to be played exists as a sort of template, which can be filled in or deconstructed as the player sees fit. Every choice is his or hers alone, so care and good taste must be applied in making decisions of style, mood, tempo, key, voicing, fretboard position, and the like. The good news is, not every decision is a difficult or challenging one. Once the player has the tools and techniques of the style under their belt, the arranging process can be distinctly exciting, leading the musician down roads that may have never even existed for them before. Taking a well known song and putting it in a drastically foreign setting—be it tempo, time signature, mood, or radical reharmonization—can be a delightfully shocking endeavor, for both the guitarist and their listeners. Not least amongst these myriad options are the new performance opportunities available to the solo jazz guitarist. At the very least, chord melody playing should give the guitarist, once fluent in the style, another way to earn a living with a guitar in their hands, be it in quiet, romantic restaurants, upscale private parties, corporate functions, or concert stages. There may be a certain fear or apprehension when first arriving at a gig entirely alone, with the responsibility of creating the evening's entertainment resting squarely on your shoulders. But once a few of these gigs are safely under the belt, stage fright will likely dissolve, to be replaced by a thrilling feeling of liberation. No more waiting for your fellow musicians to show up, late and wearing the sports jacket that spent the last week sitting at the bottom of the hamper beneath a pile of socks and underwear. No more struggling to play with the drummer who drops beats or the bassist with those funny note choices. No more attitudes and egos to deal with. And no more sharing the money! One of the beautiful things about playing music can be the camaraderie shared by fellow musicians, and the inspiration they can provide to each other. These things can never be replaced or discounted. But as a change of pace, chord melody playing can be both refreshing and challenging. And you'll be a better band guitarist because of it.

Toby Wine

ABOUT THE AUTHOR

Toby Wine is a native New Yorker and a freelance guitarist, arranger, writer, and teacher. A graduate of the Manhattan School of Music, Toby studied arranging and composition with Edward Green and the late Manny Albam. His guitar studies have included work with Ken Wessel, Bern Nix, and Chris Rosenberg, and hardcore jazz apprenticeships under saxophonist Bob Mover, and the late, legendary pianist Walter Davis Jr. Toby performs in a variety of venues throughout New York City and the Northeast, does the odd studio job, occasionally leads his own septet, quartet, and trio, and works as an arranger and musical consultant for a handful of vocalists and other performers. His compositions and arrangements can be heard on records by Philip Harper (Muse), Ari Ambrose (Steeplechase), and Ian Hendrickson-Smith (Sharp Nine & K-Pasta Records). Other career highlights include recording in the fabled Rudy Van Gelder studios in Englewood, New Jersey, and working as an orchestrator for avant-garde icon Ornette Coleman. In addition to serving as music librarian for the Carnegie Hall Jazz Band, Toby is an author, contributing writer and editor of a wide variety of books available from Cherry Lane Music. He is currently an instructor at the Church St. School for Music and Art in New York City

ACKNOWLEDGMENTS

I'd like to extend my gratitude to my editors Susan Poliniak and Mark Phillips for their guidance, patience, and insight, as well as to the entire Cherry Lane family. Also, to my parents, Rosemary and Jerry, for their infinite support and enthusiasm, and to Bibi and Bob, for their assistance and many contributions to my writing and musical careers. Thanks as well to Christina for her love, and Enid Shomer for her wisdom, and to Sam Minnitti, Tad McCully, Noah Bloom, Peter (PH-Balanced) Hartmann, Tom Hubbard, Jack S. and Jack W., Arthur Rotfeld, Chris R., Mover, Humph, Kenny, Spliff, Double-A, Philly Phil, and all the rest. You're very special to me.

GETTING STARTED

Before diving in to our chord melody meat and potatoes, we'll review various aspects of the solo jazz style, including chordal considerations, technical issues, and questions of arranging and execution. All of this is done with an eye towards understanding the eight arrangements in this book, how they were created and how they should be played, and with an eye towards the ultimate goal as well: creation of your own unique solo arrangements and repertoire. Be patient as we work our way through these elements. Even if you feel you have an excellent understanding of the subjects that follow, read them through, if only for review. You may discover something you didn't know or a new way of looking at something you do.

One more note for the fledgling chord-melodist: Listen. Grab up all the solo jazz guitar recordings you can find (Joe Pass: *Virtuoso* (Pablo Records) is the gospel according to this author, and is now available in its entirety in a four-CD set). It should be helpful to hear some of the things we'll be studying put into practice. There are magazines, newsletters, internet forums, and websites devoted to our subject as well. Many will have advice and opinions (take it or leave it!) on techniques, recordings, and publications of relevance. There are even folios and individual chord melody arrangements for sale (usually by mail order), but these should be approached with caution. There's some brilliant stuff out there, and some real dreck, and it all may be useful in helping you to get your solo jazz playing together. But in the end, you'll want to create your own arrangements and repertoire, unique music that expresses your personality in a way that something store-bought, this author's work included, can never do.

CHAPTER 1: MEMORIZING CHORD FORMS AND INVERSIONS

Chord melody playing involves the harmonization of both melody notes and improvised material, so it's essential that the solo guitarist have a wide variety of chord voicings at his or her disposal. Without a healthy assortment of chord forms safely under your fingers, arranging or improvising chord melody solos can become an interminable chore. The guitarist needs to have access to major chords with the 6th as the melody note, dominant 7ths with the ♯11 on top, minor chords leading with the 9th, and the like. A number of available books focus on just this topic, serving as encyclopedias or reference tomes of chord forms; the subject is vast enough to be impractical to examine in any truly comprehensive way amongst these pages. Instead, we'll review our most basic chord types—triads and seventh chords—in all inversions and with all chord tones serving as the lead voice. Appendix I, at the end of this book, includes all of the chords outlined in this chapter, as well as many additional voicings for use in creating your arrangements (Appendix II also contains a wealth of miscellaneous commonly encountered chords).

The following examples illustrate the five triad types (major, minor, diminished, augmented, and suspended) with each of the chord's three tones on top, as the melody note. The triads are shown on all four possible adjacent string "sets"; i.e., the E–A–D strings, A–D–G, D–G–B and G–B–E strings. Keep in mind other voicing possibilities do exist, and that the chords shown below (and the seventh chords that follow) are voiced only on adjacent strings, without skipping. It's entirely possible to play a C major chord utilizing the low E string, with the D and B strings on top, but an examination of such possibilities belongs in a major reference work dedicated to that nearly infinite topic alone. Another note: instead of showing the inversions in purely ascending fashion, we have occasionally dropped them down an octave to minimize ledger lines and keep them on the meat of the neck and not far above the 12th fret, where they will doubtless be infrequently needed.

Triads on the E–A–D Strings

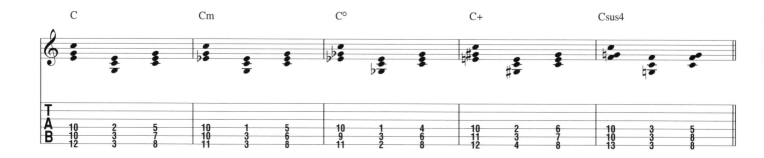

Triads on the A–D–G Strings

Triads on the D–G–B Strings

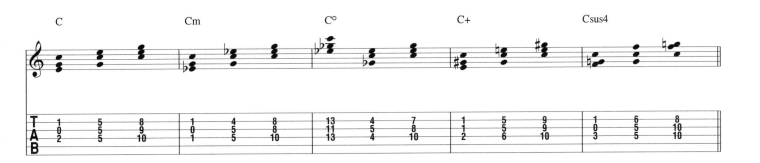

Triads on the G–B–E Strings

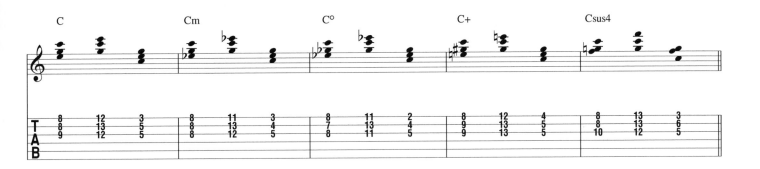

The examples below illustrate the basic seventh chords—major, minor, dominant, minor seventh flat-five (or half-diminished, as it's often called) and fully diminished—in all inversions, on the three possible sets of four adjacent strings, just like the triads we've just examined. Both three and four-note chord types of all qualities and inversions should be studied and practiced like any other material until they are memorized and instantly accessible. You'll want them both under your fingers and in your ears. Remember, these voicings represent the mere tip of the iceberg in terms of the chords that are not only possible, but essential to know.

Seventh Chords on the E–A–D–G Strings

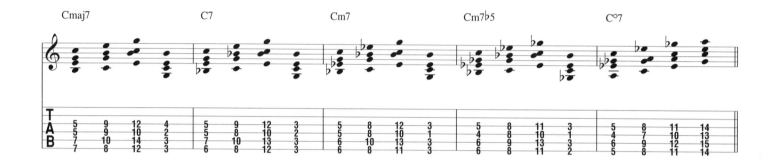

Seventh Chords on the A–D–G–B Strings

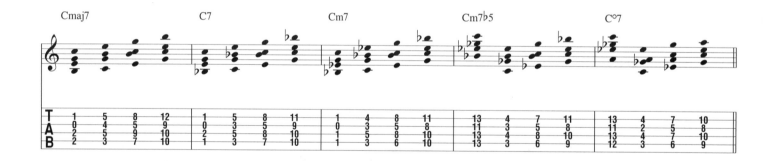

Seventh Chords on the D–G–B–E Strings

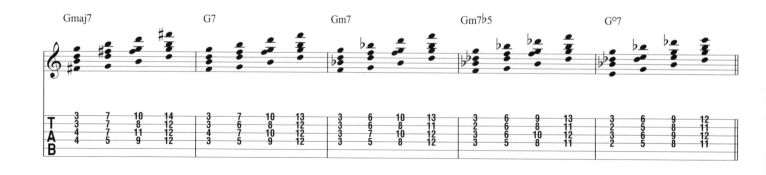

If you've spent time practicing your arpeggios, you should already have a good idea of how to work on the previous chords and their inversions. Working very slowly, select one of the triads or seventh chord types, then play it with the root, third, fifth, and seventh as the melody note, before descending back to where you began. This will give you the fully harmonized arpeggio for each of these chord types. Use a metronome and acclimate yourself slowly to the shifts between voicings. Always be aware of the chord type you're playing and which tone is serving as the lead voice. This kind of practice involves both muscle memory and an awareness of the theory behind what you're playing, so it's useful to keep both the physical and mental aspects in mind as you work. You may also want to isolate one or two chord voicings that may be giving you particular trouble, and just work on shifting back and forth between them slowly until they begin to feel comfortable.

Let's reiterate for a moment: the voicings shown so far represent only a fraction of what is not only possible but utterly necessary. We may have memorized major seventh chords on all string sets with the root, third, fifth, and seventh on top, but how about when the melody note is the ninth or the thirteenth? The topic is virtually infinite. As you read through and work on the eight arrangements presented later in this book, take note of the chord voicings encountered, the chord type (or chord *quality*), and what the melody note is in relation to the chord's root. The preceding voicings do not include some of the more exotic chord types either: complex sounds such as augmented major sevenths, diminished or minor chords with major 7ths, altered dominant-sevenths, unusual suspensions, and poly- or "slash" chords, (C/D, E♭maj7/A, etc.). Lastly, you'll find the arrangements chock full of chords comprised of stacked 4ths, which can usually be played with a bar to allow other fingers to execute walking bass lines or upper register melodies while the meat of the chord continues to ring. Often (but not always), chords with extensions in the lead voice will be structured in this way and may be encountered without roots, a sound that may be somewhat ambiguous at first but should become more familiar in context, among other more traditional voicings. The examples show how 4th chords can be used to harmonize both a C major scale and C Dorian mode. Take note of the way they're employed when you play through the songs that follow.

Major and Dorian Scales with Stacked 4ths

Harmonized C Major Scale on the A–D–G–B Strings

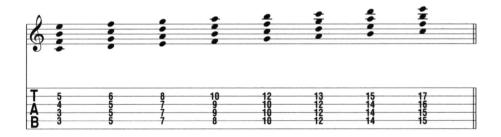

Harmonized C Dorian Scale on the A–D–G–B Strings

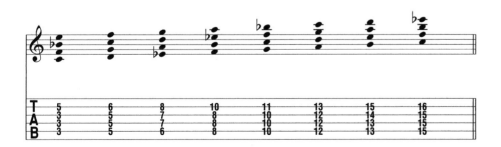

CHAPTER 2: JAZZ PROGRESSIONS AND SUBSTITUTIONS

One of the primary concerns of the chord-melody guitarist is the chord progressions of the song at hand and what to do with them. It should prove to be a rare scenario wherein you'll find they need no tweaking at all, and this will most likely be in the case of real jazz tunes: work by composers like Chick Corea, John Coltrane, or Thelonious Monk (as opposed to the standards of the Tin Pan Alley composers). The music produced by these men and others like them is usually so finely detailed and fully realized that their songs will stand on their own and usually make a fool of you if you try to make them hipper than they already are. But other composers, most often the authors of our cherished standards, have penned songs that leave much more room for reinterpretation and reinvigoration. Much of the work of the jazz musician/composer is too dense harmonically, too specific rhythmically and melodically, to offer much chance for an overhaul. This is, of course, a broad generalization, but the old-school songwriters often wrote for vocalists, precluding melodic lines full of rapid eighth notes and large intervallic leaps; much of their work, the meat of the jazz canon, is now decades old and was produced prior to many of the harmonic innovations their interpreters wrought in the years that followed.

So, where then to begin? Start with this philosophy: add only that which makes the music stronger, remove only that which weakens it. The task then becomes identifying the essential harmonic components of a song, the dominant-to-tonic cadences, key changes and the like, and the non-essential chords and filler that serve little or no purpose in the grand scheme of things. If you're learning standards from one of those old, two-staff piano fakebooks with guitar chord pictograms, you're gonna find a lot of filler. These chord charts rarely reflect the composer's original chords accurately and may have been put together by folks without a jazz guitar background. Regardless, one of the best methods of understanding harmonic progressions is what is commonly referred to as *Roman numeral analysis*. If you're unfamiliar with this approach, it's urgently recommended that you familiarize yourself with it, whether through independent study in music theory or with a teacher or good textbook. Fundamentally, each note of our diatonic (major) scale—the most basic building block of nearly all Western music—has a corresponding chord of specific quality when stacked in 3rds.

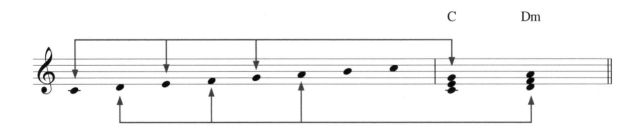

As you can see, by combining the 1st, 3rd, and 5th notes of the C major scale, we produce a C major triad. Combining the 2nd, 4th, and 6th notes of the same scale results in a D minor triad.

If we follow the same approach up the scale, we create major, minor, and in the case of the seventh degree of the scale, diminished triads. The final result is a properly corresponding chord for each scale degree, in sequence: major, minor, minor, major, major, minor, diminished. These can now be referred to as the I chord, the ii chord, the iii chord, and so on (major chords are given upper case Roman numerals, minor and diminished chords are given lower case). If we say a tune has a I–vi–ii–V progression in the key of C, we mean the C major, A minor, D minor, and G major chords. In the key of A♭, the chords in this progression would be A♭ major, F minor, B♭ minor, and E♭ major. These formulas and relationships remain consistent in every key.

Now let's add a fourth note to each chord:

We've created seventh chords, with a few big changes occurring: the V chord is now a dominant seventh chord and no longer a mere major triad, and the chord built on the seventh degree of the scale has been transformed from a diminished triad to a minor seventh flat-five chord—also called a "half-diminished" (a subtler but nevertheless still important distinction we'll get back to shortly). The relationship between tonic (I) chord and dominant (V7) chord is doubtless the most important in all of Western music. V7–I is the most commonly encountered chord progression, and each note in the dominant chord possesses a strong, almost gravitational pull towards a tone in the tonic chord. The dominant creates tension and the tonic provides resolution.

The following three cadences illustrate the movement of the individual voices in the chords of this progression. Regardless of inversion or voicing, the 3rd of the dominant seventh chord will always seek to rise to the root of the I chord (B to C), and its ♭7th will always pull down to the 3rd of the I chord (F to E).

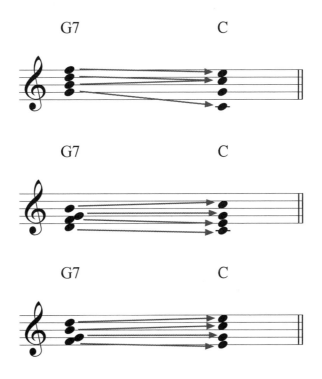

We spoke earlier about the elimination of non-essential chords, but it's common practice in jazz writing and playing (as well as in certain pop tunes) to insert a ii minor seventh chord immediately preceding a V–I cadence, making the ii–V–I the most frequently occurring chord progression in the style. These "ii–V's" appear almost constantly in mainstream jazz and are used in both diatonic (single-key) progressions and as bridges between various keys whenever changes occur. Examine the progression below:

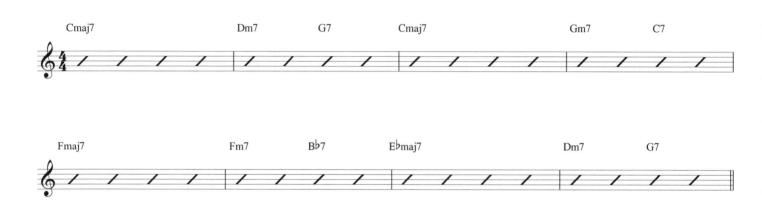

This typical progression includes three key changes, moving to the key of the IV (F), the ♭III (E♭), and returning to the original key. The Fmaj7 chord is the IV in the key of C, but it temporarily becomes the I chord because it's preceded by Gm7 and C7 chords, two chords found not in the key of C but in the key of F. A harmonic analysis of such a progression would look like this:

$$\text{I / ii V / I / ii V of IV / IV / ii V of } ♭\text{III / } ♭\text{III / ii V}$$

By analyzing chord movement in this way, we get a better understanding of what's happening harmonically, especially in more complex or confusing progressions. We can also get a clearer picture of a chord's function—is it a non-diatonic chord that connects diatonic changes, or is it a true key shift? Let's consider the following three examples.

In the chord progression above, the E♭7 chord exists outside of the key of C but serves as a chromatic bridge between Em7 and Dm7. It doesn't move into the key from which it was borrowed (the key of A♭). We'd analyze the progression like this:

$$\text{iii } ♭\text{III7 / ii V / I}$$

Our second example above follows the I chord with a ii V in the key of Eb, the bIII in the home key. Rather than resolving to Eb major, the progression returns to C and moves down with a passing chord (Bb7) to the VI chord, which has been converted from a minor to dominant seventh quality (a common practice we'll examine shortly). A Roman numeral analysis would read:

$$I \ / \ ii \ V \ of \ \flat III \ / \ I \ \flat VII7 \ / \ VI7$$

In the final example above, we get major help from the key signature that reveals we're in Eb. The meaning of the chords can be unclear, so we backtrack from the tonic in the 3rd measure and find that it's preceded by its V, then by a Gmaj7 chord preceded by its own V, then by a Bmaj7 chord. This is a tune that is clearly jumping around from key to key, as evidenced by the V–I resolutions that connect the B, G, and Eb chords. An admittedly complex Roman numeral analysis would read:

$$\flat VImaj7 \ / \ V \ of \ IIImaj7 \ / \ IIImaj7 \ V \ / \ I$$

The distinction between key changes, which are major harmonic events and should rarely—if ever—be changed or omitted, and non-diatonic chords that occur in otherwise diatonic settings (passing chords) is an important one indeed. Take out any fake book and do as much Roman numeral analysis as you can stand—your understanding of harmony, songwriting, and the like will be greatly enhanced in the long run.

We've already said that it's common practice to put the ii in front of the V. The essence of what's happening is the resolution of V to I (or the avoidance of it), but the ii has merit of its own. The inner voices of the chords move in a strong fashion that helps to emphasize the tension and resolution between dominant and tonic:

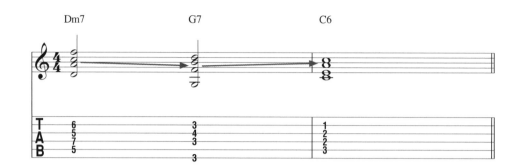

The C in the Dm7 chord moves down to the B in the G7 chord before rising again, in closure, to the C that is the tonic of the C6 chord. Single line soloists outline this motion as well:

Track 1 contains tuning pitches.

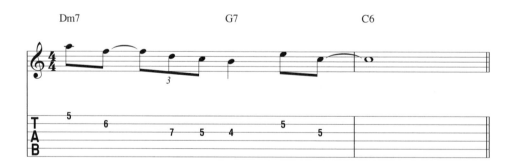

A Guide to Chord-Melody Jazz Guitar

So, what else happens in the "jazzification" of a standard tune? Two of the most common substitutions are the changing of the vi minor chord to a dominant seventh, and the tritone substitution. In the first case, the vi minor in a major key–song will almost always become a dominant seventh when it's followed by the ii chord. The vi effectively becomes the "V of ii." Even if the melody doesn't permit this—a rarity—the change will be made during the solo choruses.

For example, this:

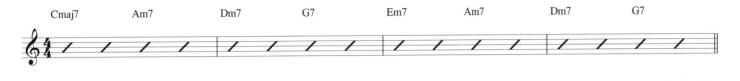

becomes this:

All of the Am7 chords have been changed to A7ths. The VI7 will frequently be converted into an altered dominant seventh chord because two of its characteristic extensions, the ♯9 and ♭13, are notes that also exist in the key's parent scale (in the key of C, an A7 ♯9/♭13 chord would include both C and F tones—the 1st and 4th degrees in the home key). Another little tweak of the progression happens in the final measure, where the second Dm7 has been changed to D7. Many songs already have a II7 built in ("Take the 'A' Train," for example), but it works here as a sort of "V of V," the dominant seventhchord in relation to G. It doesn't really matter that the G is a dominant seventh chord and not a major chord—it's all about "fiveing" or "two-fiveing" wherever you go. Almost any chord in jazz can be preceded by its dominant seventh; it's just a matter of discretion and taste whether you use this device at any given time or not.

The tritone substitution is another very common device in jazz. Basically, it exchanges one dominant seventh chord for another that's a tritone (♭5th) away, giving you all kinds of comping and soloing options, and creating interesting and more highly chromatic root (bass) movement. Take any two dominant seventh chords a tritone apart, compare their pitches, and you'll find they're pretty much the same chord in that they share common thirds and sevenths, the most important parts of any chord in terms of harmonic function:

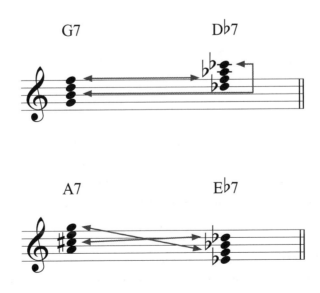

The arrows in the previous examples indicate the common notes between the two chords. The G7 and Db7 chords share both F and B pitches (naming the seventh of Db7 as a "Cb" for enharmonic correctness), and the A7 and Eb7 chords share their C♯ and G pitches (the C♯ becomes Db in an Eb7 chord). So, any time you have a dominant seventh chord, it can be exchanged for its tritone relation, although you may have to tweak any extensions if the melody dictates.

Lets take this simple little phrase:

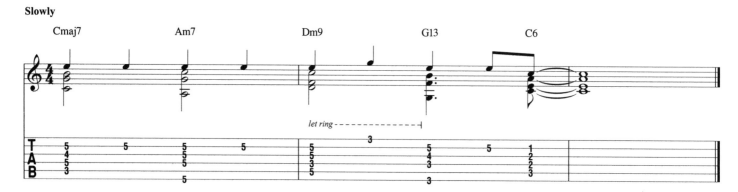

and change it to this:

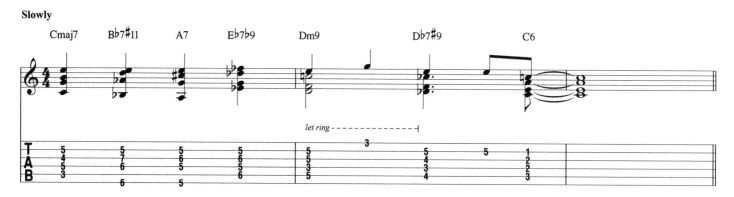

A lot has happened in the second incarnation, so follow carefully. The Am7 chord, which has been changed to an A7 (this is sometimes called "modal interchange": the root stays the same, but the chord type and corresponding scale or mode has been changed), is now preceded by a Bb7♯11, a chromatic passing chord. The Eb7 chord that follows is the tritone sub of A7; the Dm9 chord remains the same. Keep in mind, too much substitution can quickly become overkill and negate the impact of those more unusual chords, something this example is very near to doing.

The final substitution swaps Db7♯9 for G13, the tritone sub of the V chord in C major, and allows for a nicely chromatic D–Db–C movement in the bass. Notice that what was the 13th of G13 has now become the ♯9 of Db7♯9, an example of the kind of transformation chord extensions undergo in the tritone substitution process. Look for opportunities of your own to apply these types of subs to your playing, arranging, and composing, and pay attention when they occur in the arranged standards presented later in this book.

Before we veer too far away from the subject at hand, take a look at the two choruses of minor blues that follow and identify the tritone subs, other alterations, and their functions:

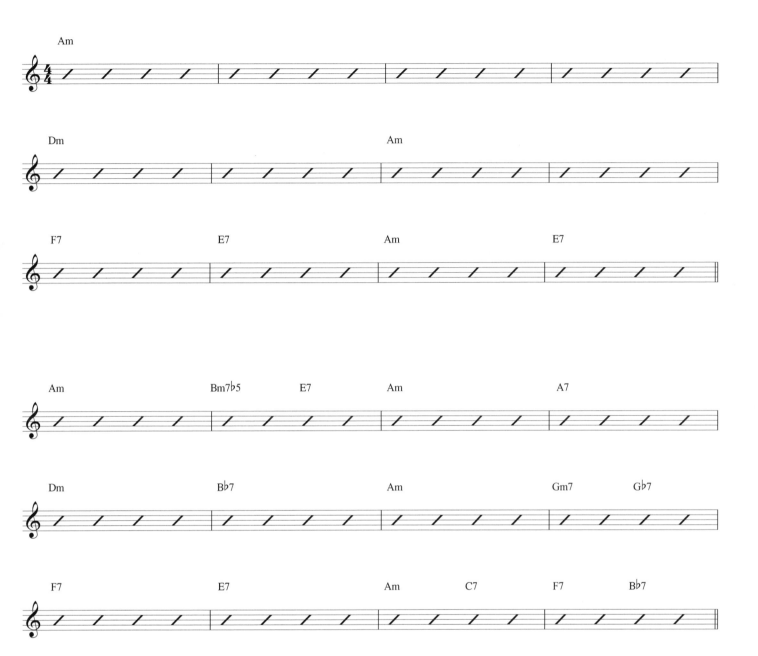

Earlier, we said that the 7th degree of the major scale became a diminished triad when harmonized, and became a minor seventh flat-five chord (or half-diminished) when a fourth note is added. The minor seventh flat-five chord is nearly always used as the "ii" in a ii–V–i to a minor chord. Take this example, the first four measures of "Come Rain or Come Shine":

The progression begins on the I chord in the key of F and is followed by the vii, III, vi, and II chords. However, the second measure temporarily leaves the key of F and enters the realm of its relative minor (D minor) by virtue of the A7 chord—the "V of vi." The vii chord in the home key, Em7♭5, serves as the ii of D minor in this case. The II chord in the final measure is G7 (a "secondary dominant") rather than Gm7, another common practice whose function is as a "V of V." But minor seventh flat-five, diminished triads, and fully diminished seventh chords (in which the seventh degree is *doubly flatted* and becomes a major sixth) have another important function. Each of these types of chords can serve the role of a dominant seventh chord *in inversion*. The fully diminished chord almost always functions in this way. Look at the similarity between G7 and theses diminished types:

The Bm7♭5 is identical save for the exchange of G for A, the major 9th of a G7 chord. The B diminished triad (and its inversions, D and F diminished triads) has the same pitches as G7 except for the root, G. And the four diminished seventh chords (all merely inversions of each other) use the same notes as well, only exchanging the G for an A♭, the ♭9th of a G7 chord. So any dominant seventh chord can be replaced by a diminished triad or seventh chord built on its 3rd, 5th, 7th, and ♭9th degrees, and by a minor seventh flat-five chord built on its 3rd or 7th. Take this example, a sequence found in numerous standards:

The C♯°7 chord is actually, functionally, an A7♭9 with its 3rd in the bass—the V of ii. And the D♯°7 chord works as a B7♭9 in the same way, as the V of iii. Soloists usually approach this sequence with that in mind, playing lines built on A7 and B7 rather than from C♯ and D♯ diminished scales.

Take a look at these two "A" sections of "rhythm" changes in B♭:

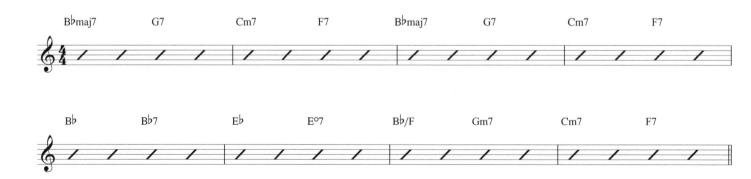

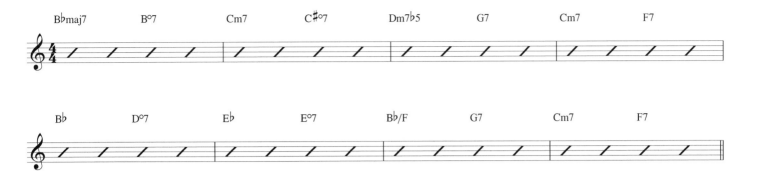

The first eight measures are about as "inside" as this progression is played. In the second version, we find the ascending sequence we observed earlier, with the B°7 and C♯°7 chords functioning as the V of ii and V of iii, respectively. The iii chord is often substituted for I and can be a minor seventh or minor seventh flat-five chord, depending on taste and the surrounding harmonic and melodic context. Measure 5 of our example finds us subbing D°7 for B♭7 (the V of IV), and the E°7 acts like a C7 chord, the V of V (F). Gm7 in measure seven becomes G7 the second time (the V of ii), but could easily be B, D, F, or A♭ diminished seventh chords as well.

The diminished chord is really one of the deepest and most complex of all musical riddles. Look at some of your favorite tunes, see how the diminished chords are used and where they can be substituted for dominant chords to create variety and more interesting root movement. The diminished scale (in C: C–D–E♭–F–G♭–A♭–A♮–B) contains a wide variety of triads and patterns that have long been favorite playthings for sophisticated soloists. Classical composers (not known for "two-fiving" from key to key) have also used the diminished scale as a bridge between remote keys in place of a dominant chord, as in this example that skips from G to D♭ to B to G:

TRACK 05

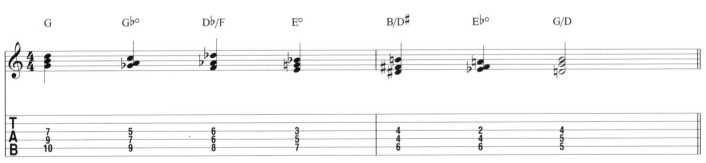

Play around with that for a while. And let's not neglect another function of the diminished, its use as a delay before a tonic chord. The diminished chord built on the tonic of the home key works when the melody note is a root, 6th, 9th, or 7th (as in our arrangements of "Misty" and "Call Me Irresponsible" featured later in this book). It's just one of many devices used to avoid resolution to the "I" that are found in all musical styles. Others include moving to the iii minor seventh or minor seventh flat-five in lieu of the I chord (as the beginning of a iii–VI7–ii–V7 turnaround), or "deceptive cadences" that resolve to chords taken from the parallel minor key (in C major, these would most frequently be C minor and A♭, B♭, and E♭ major chords). You'll encounter many of these in the arrangements that follow this discussion.

Harmonic rhythm—the rate and frequency that the harmony changes, or that chords go by—is an important consideration when writing, arranging, or substituting. A song that goes for long stretches with only one chord per measure, or in any predictable pattern, will quickly become uninteresting. Something like "rhythm" changes works because the "A" sections are crammed with two chords per measure (two beats each), but the bridge opens up with each chord lasting a full two measures (eight beats each)—the contrast is very strong. If the song you're arranging has few chords, spice it up by making a couple of select measures denser with substitutions. If it's really busy, see what could be taken out to create contrast. Chords that don't really serve any harmonic function are the most likely candidates. In an old-fashioned fake book, you're likely to find something like this:

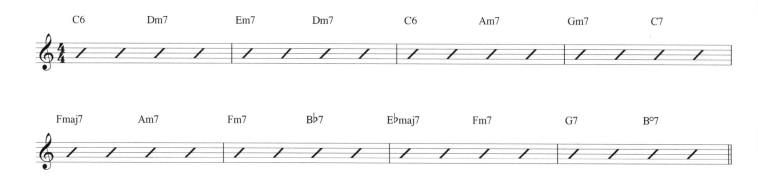

This is a lousy progression, for a couple of reasons. First, its harmonic rhythm is predictable and repetitive, with two chords to every bar without variation. Secondly, there's a lot of waste, harmonically speaking, with a number of chords that serve little or no harmonic function. So, how can we fix it? Here's one way:

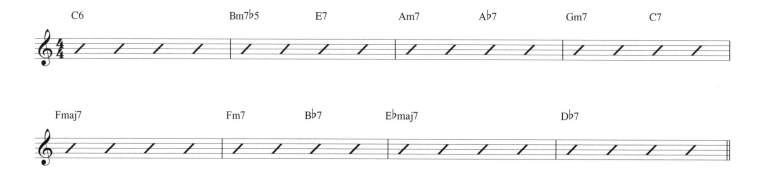

Keep in mind that this is one of dozens of possible solutions, and that it doesn't take into account any melody that might be written over the original changes. But we're talking strictly about chord progressions and harmonic rhythm here, so let's see what's happened. The Dm7, Em7, Dm7 sequence that follows the tonic chord in the first two measures is common enough, and is often applied to a situation where the tonic chord remains static for a few measures. Basically, it gives the bass something to do but creates nothing essential harmonically. The Am7 chords in measures 3 and 5 provide little that isn't already contained in the chords that precede them, and actually weaken the root movement—the bass jumps down a third after moving in stepwise fashion both before and after, so the ear misses hearing a "B" connecting "C" and "A." The Fmaj7 chord in measure 5 jumps up a third to Am7 and back down again to Fm7, a completely wasted motion by the bass. And, in the example's final measure, B°7 is a synonym for G7♭9, so it contributes little but the bass movement inevitably leading back to the tonic.

What's really going on in this progression is movement from the home key (C) to the key of the IV (F) and the ♭III (E♭) before returning home in the final measure (V7 of I). So instead of the diatonic stuff in the first three measures, we target the Fmaj7 chord and work backwards in a series of ii–V's: Gm7–C7 is the ii–V of F; Am7–A♭7 is a ii–V (with a tritone sub!) to G, and Bm7♭5–E7 is a ii–V of A minor. Combine that with an entire measure of Cmaj7 at the beginning and things are much more interesting already. We remove the Am7 and Fm7 chords in measures 5 and 7, respectively, eliminating waste and making the harmonic rhythm stronger. G7/B°7 in the final measure becomes D♭7, a tritone sub, and improves the flow of things as well by not following each measure of one chord with a measure containing two.

Let's wrap up our intro to jazz arranging by looking first at the chorus of "Jingle Bells" with its most basic chords, then arrange the same excerpt for chord melody guitar with a handful of the many substitutions and techniques we've just examined.

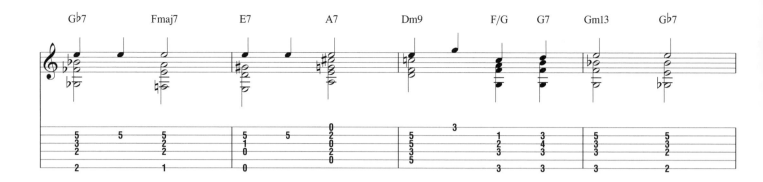

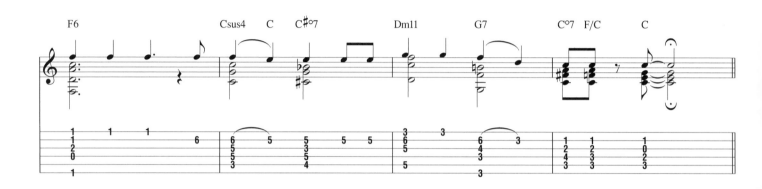

CHAPTER 3: BASS LINES AND ROOT MOVEMENT

The chord melody guitarist assumes the responsibility of an entire band, providing melody, harmony, rhythm, and bass parts. Integrating walking bass lines with chords and single-note ideas can be challenging but it's a technique that becomes easier and more instinctual with practice. The first thing to remember is that it isn't necessary to have an unbroken quarter note pulse at all times. If chords and lines are played in a swinging, propulsive fashion, it's often enough to interject a walking line here and there to keep the groove going when things in the upper registers are held or rested. In the arrangements that follow, you'll find walking bass lines used sporadically to keep the momentum going or fill in the spaces, but not providing the sole impetus to swing. In this section, we'll look at a blues in Bb in three different incarnations: with walking bass alone, with a combination of chords and bass lines, and finally with chords, bass, and solo lines simultaneously.

The melody or "head" sections of a tune will often provide most of the answers on their own in terms of when and how to use bass lines. Many of your chords will have the root in the bass, which makes the task a question of connecting one root to another with chord tones or chromatic passing notes. But solo sections that you may want to build into an arrangement will benefit by more extensive bass work, allowing you to keep the groove going while you interject short, punchy chords or flowing eighth note lines. Some general principles to keep in mind when constructing walking bass parts, whether composed or improvised, are:

1. Try to use chord tones (the root, 3rd, 5th, and 7th) on beats one and three in 4/4 time, and other scale or chromatic passing tones on beats two and four.

2. A bassist can turn the beat around with their quarter notes merely by playing pitches on the wrong beat. If you keep landing on the root of a chord on beat four, it's going to eventually feel like the downbeat.

3. It's okay to break up the quarter note pulse with triplets, eighth notes, or longer rhythmic values, but don't overdo it. Constant variation can detract from the overall swing or groove and make things feel herky-jerky or give them a stop-start quality. You may want to go for this effect on occasion, but you'll usually want to create a sense of smooth and seamless time and the transitions from bass to chords to solo lines. Remember, there isn't any drummer there to keep the time together, so you'll have to assume some of his role as well.

4. Be sure you know how to arpeggiate each chord in the progression and what the proper corresponding scale is (i.e.: a D°7 chord indicates the notes D, F, A, and C, and is derived from the D Dorian (D-E-F-G-A-B-C) or D Aeolian (D-E-F-G-A-Bb-C) modes).

5. Practice walking through various chord progressions in one left hand position—this is a terrific exercise for chord playing and soloing as well. Take any tune you like, begin anywhere on the neck, and stay there as chords and keys change. This will get you deeper inside the harmony and the fingerboard and get you away from "box" playing or jumping all over the neck. Ideally, we'd play the whole guitar, from top to bottom, but it's a lot of wasted motion when you *have* to jump to the 10th fret every time you're playing a D chord. Here are two examples of this approach, applied to the first four measures of "My Romance:"

TRACK 08

TRACK 09

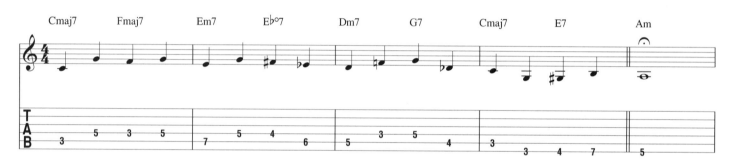

6. Pay attention to your right hand attack, be it with pick or fingers. Many players find it easier to play chords and bass lines without the pick, using the thumb for the bass parts and the other fingers to grab chords simultaneously. You'll get a warmer, more bass-like sound down below, and grabbing chords lets you sound each voice at precisely the same instant, something that's next to impossible to do with a pick. You'll also be able to exert pinpoint dynamic control over each chord tone as well, allowing you to emphasize or de-emphasize any voice you choose. The trade-off is that many players are less comfortable playing fast single-note lines without a pick, so it's not all good. A common solution is to palm the pick or hold it between fingers when you don't need it; this can work very well but can also be a lot of effort if it isn't second nature to the player. Another approach is a kind of hybrid picking, where the thumb and forefinger hold the pick and the remaining fingers do any work on the upper strings—again, a fairly specialized technique. If you do use a pick for walking bass lines, strike the strings relatively lightly and with an even attack—you want to sound like an acoustic bassist, and pick noise isn't going to help!

7. Keep the principles of strong root movement in mind. We touched on the subject in the previous chapter; all of the rules and techniques of chord substitution apply to the bass parts as well (e.g. the use of diminished seventh chords as subs for dominant seventh chords, etc.). Avoid anything too jarring, such as frequent jumps from register to register or anything else that might break up the continuity of a good line. You want to create a nicely rounded contour, not a collection of jagged peaks and valleys. Think arpeggios and scale tones at first, with scalar or chromatic passing tones used as connectors from chord to chord. Look at these two examples of walking bass lines for the first four measures of "Come Rain or Come Shine:"

TRACK 10

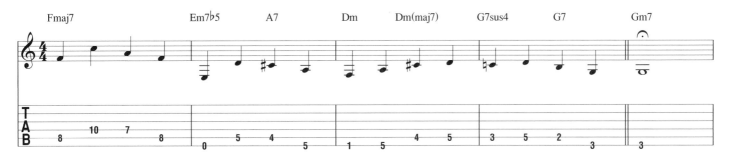

TRACK 11

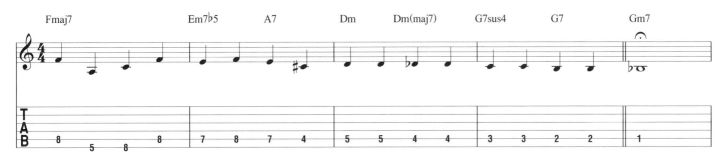

The first example is a mess, while the second is very strong. Why? In the first case, there are number of jarring leaps and drops (down a minor 9th from F to E at the end of measure one, up a minor 7th from E to D in measure two). Roots fall on beat four in each measure, something that will eventually get a ride cymbal thrown at your head. Repeated notes can be quite good, but not the way they're shown here, with the same pitch (G) on both beat four and one consecutively! These are mere guidelines, and you're allowed to take any risks you like, as the best players do, but until you've got the fundamentals together and the experience to know a good note choice and a lousy one, stick to the basics.

The second example is conservative but nicely constructed. Chord tones fall on beats one and three throughout, movement from chord to chord is scalar (F to E) or chromatic (C♯ to D), and the repeated notes in the final two measures (dividing each measure in half—never falling on beats two and three!) provide a nice contrast to the earlier measures while outlining the inner voice-leading of the chord changes. We said earlier that the third of a dominant seventh chord always seeks to rise to the root of its I chord; the C# rising to D in measure two lets it happen instead of fighting musical gravity.

8. Keep things interesting. Much like comping, you don't want to fall into predictable, repetitive patterns with your bass lines. Change directions frequently, don't play the root on every downbeat (try a different chord tone instead) and avoid using the same chromatic connections for every chord change. Walking bass is an art as complex as any other in jazz; practice it on a variety of tunes and keep all of the above principles in mind. If you really want an education, get out your favorite records and transcribe the lines of different bass players, taking note of what they do differently and what they all have in common in terms of approach.

Finally, lets look at those three choruses of B♭ blues I mentioned at the beginning of this discussion. Begin by playing through the first, constructed of walking bass lines alone:

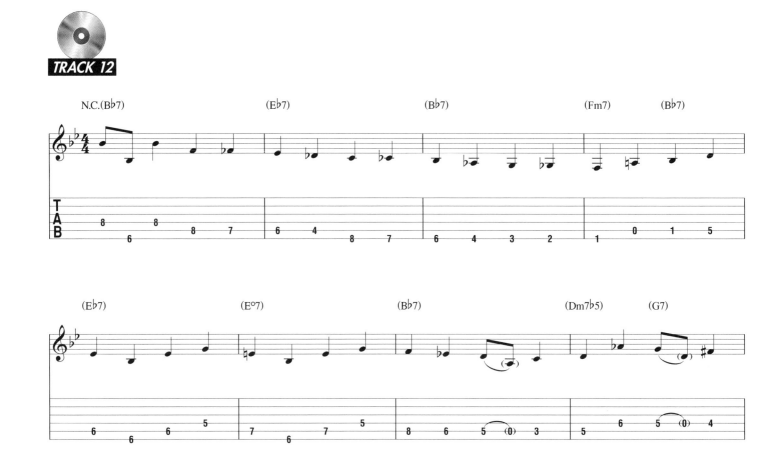

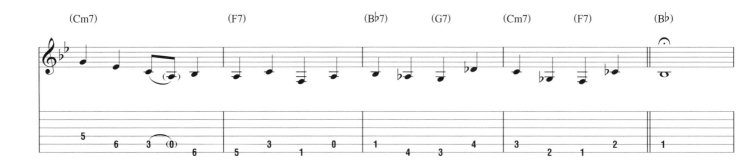

That should be fairly simple and straightforward by now. Notice the infrequent use of eighth notes, most of which are subtle pull-offs to open strings that imitate the sound and style of an acoustic bassist.

A Guide to Chord-Melody Jazz Guitar

Now, let's add some chords:

TRACK 13

As you can see, it isn't necessary to pack every measure with chords in order to get a clear picture of the harmony, especially if you do a good job of outlining what's happening with your bass line. This example keeps things interesting by staying away from patterns and placing chords on upbeats and quarter notes, and by letting some ring while others are short stabs of punctuation. Notice the use of chromatic "approach" chords as well (C♭7–B♭7, G♭m7–Fm7, etc.), another typical device of the style.

Now, lets put it all together with some single-note soloing:

TRACK 14

This example takes a little soloing, some chords, and a walking bass line to fill in the gaps, all without doing too much or becoming extremely difficult to play. Take your time in these situations and keep it simple. The whole process eventually becomes instinctual, but all three musical levels you're working on must be under your control both technically and theoretically. If you're unclear about what scale goes with each chord or how to play a Db13b9, you're going to stumble because it will quickly become too much to think about at once. When creating a repertoire of original chord melody arrangements, you'll probably want to leave space in most to take a solo or two, so practice "blowing" on the tunes you like with chords, bass lines, single-note runs, and combinations of the three. Work slowly, and you'll soon be doing it all once. You'll be a better ensemble guitarist as well, as your ears will be attuned to hearing the bass and chordal accompaniment in greater detail, and you won't need to rely on a pianist or second guitarist to provide chords for your solos.

CHAPTER 4: STYLE POINTS: SINGLE-NOTE LINES AND FILLS, RUBATO PLAYING, CHROMATICISM AND MORE

You've chosen a tune, learned its melody and chords, considered substitutions and bass lines. Now's the time to put your creativity to the test by adding the smaller details that will give your arrangement some personality. Let's go over a few ideas for adding style and flair:

1. Consider the overall setting of the tune by choosing a key, tempo and mood that you like. Try to keep your repertoire as varied as possible to keep yourself and your listeners involved and excited. Avoid programming (either in performance or recording) consecutive songs in the same key. Experiment with swing, latin (Samba, Bossa Nova, Bolero, etc.), and straight eighth note grooves. Arrangements can touch on multiple keys (see the arrangement of "Misty" that follows), time signatures ("Call Me Irresponsible"), and tempos (using rubato or double and half time shifts, to name a few).

2. Try to retain the detailed phrasing you would use when soloing in a band context. Slurs, slides, hammer-ons, and vibrato are just a few of the many techniques we use to add expressiveness to our playing. You'll have a lot more responsibility in a solo context, but don't forget these vital tools that transform mere notes into living, breathing music.

3. Create interesting intros and endings. You may wish to tackle these after you've come up with the bulk of the arrangement; pieces of melody, chordal passages, or other thematic material can provide ideas to make the chore easier. In the end, you can take your cues from the song—as in our arrangement of "Come Fly with Me"—or compose something altogether new, such as the intros to "My Favorite Things" and "Call Me Irresponsible." Many arrangers fashion intros and endings from turnarounds and other chord sequences, as in our arrangements of "Alfie" and "My Romance."

4. Re-use of thematic material is an important technique in arranging and composing. As mentioned above, pieces of melody or sequences of chords that are particularly striking can be used again in a variety of ways, and can serve as a unifying force in your arrangement. If you've got a musical tidbit that's exceptionally hip or beautiful, don't let it go to waste by using it only once. Better to make good use of a small assortment of ideas than to try and cram every trick you can think of into one arrangement. If you're serious about creating a chord melody repertoire, you'll find a way to get them all in eventually.

5. Many solo performers are fond of rubato playing, and it's used in intros, first sections, as a way of going in and out of time, or throughout a complete arrangement. Contrary to what many think, rubato is not merely rhythmless notes or lack of any discernible tempo. Instead, rubato allows us to take our time on the pretty phrases, hold those special notes of particular power or emotion, and hurry up or slow down as the song or our mood dictates. It's a deceptively complex art and one that takes time to develop, as it's largely intuitive. Certain passages will suggest a speed or appropriate pacing, but much of rubato playing must come from the player's unique tastes and sensibility. Try singing through the section away from your instrument and imagine how you'd like it to sound. Listen to singers and their accompaniment, as well as other solo guitarists and some of the many solo jazz piano recordings. Modern chord melody players have fashioned much of their approach after the great solo pianists, who often contrast swinging numbers with slower, ruminative songs filled with rubato passages and cascading single-note phrases. Take a look at the rubato sections in the arrangements of "Misty" and "Alfie" to see some of the ways this important approach can be utilized.

6. Single-note lines and riffs can play a vital part in adding interest and excitement to your arrangements. Look for opportunities to slip a fleet run in here or there—rests and places where chords or melody slow down or stop can provide these little windows of opportunity. Consider these examples, first from "Misty," then from "Take the 'A' Train":

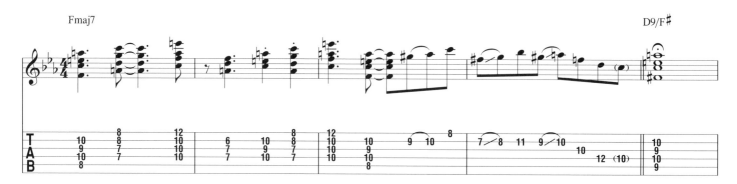

The excerpt from "Misty," which covers the first four measures of any "A" section, shows how much space is afforded to slip in some single-note lines on slow tempos and ballads. The effect can be quite seamless if carefully done, connecting chord, melody, and solo parts into one unified whole. It's best to insert these lines gradually, however—especially on a tender ballad. Single-note lines can increase the flow and swing of your arrangement, but can also make it feel cluttered if used injudiciously. Note the tritone substitution of A7#11 for Eb9 in measure 2 as well.

The "A Train" excerpt shows the same technique applied to the first four measures of the song's bridge. On faster tempos, these little solo lines can really help to ratchet up the swing quotient while alleviating some of the need to play a chord or bass line in every measure.

7. The solo lines in the previous two examples are chock full of passing (non-scalar) tones that serve as "chromatic connectors" between chord and scale notes. Modern jazz playing utilizes these chromatic tones extensively in all parts of the music, including solos, chords, and bass lines. We've already discussed the manner in which they can be used in walking bass lines to connect roots and chord tones (the root, 3rd, 5th, and 7th) and extensions (the 9th, 11th, 13th, and their alterations). Any study of jazz soloing techniques (through books, recordings, and transcription) will reveal how they're used in precisely the same way in single-note lines. But they're equally effective in chord playing as well. Take the following excerpt from "Come Fly with Me," the fifth through eighth measures of the "A" section:

TRACK 17

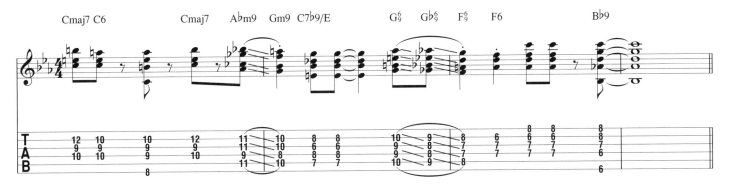

We can take advantage of the chromatic nature of the melody by using sliding, parallel chord voicings to shadow it. In the first measure, the chromatic note, B♭, slides down to A♮ in the following measure, the 9th of a Gm9 chord. So we put an A♭m9 chord before it, and the whole thing slides down together. The end of the second measure has an A♭ as the chromatic passing note between A♮ and G♮. The target chord here is the F6/9 at the beginning of measure 3, so we slide down chromatically from G to G♭ to F, with the 9th (the melody note) on top of each chord. Take note as well of the E°7 chord shape that functions as C7♭9 in measure 2, a common substitution we discussed earlier.

There are other, nearly infinite ways to use chromatic chords as well. Let's go back to "Misty" for a moment:

TRACK 18

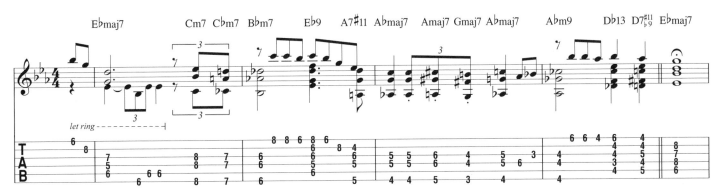

Here, chromatic chords (Cm7, C♭m7) are used to push down to a targeted chord (B♭m7) in the first measure. In measure 3, we "orbit" the IV chord, A♭maj7, with chords both a half-step above and below to create motion and fill space. And in measure 4, D7♯11♭9 becomes the chromatic connector between D♭13 and E♭maj7, a lovely bit of motion that harmonizes the melody note richly. As you work your way through the arrangements in this book, carefully note the use of chromaticism in bass lines, single-note runs, and chordal applications like the ones we've just highlighted. Discover ways to apply them to your own playing and arranging. Like any other musical technique, it's easy to overdo it—chromatic passing notes and chords will be more effective if used sparingly, where they'll stand out in contrast to diatonic material. If your arrangement is swimming in a sea of chromaticism, passing notes will lose their impact quickly.

8. Pay attention to the voice leading (or lack of it) in your chordal arranging. Voice leading is merely the flow and continuity of each individual note as you move from chord to chord. As guitarists, it's easy to forget, but chords are not blocks of sound, hand positions, or memorized shapes on the fretboard. Rather, they are collections of individual voices that are sounded together to produce harmony. Most classical musicians can't sit down with a fake book and play the chord progressions therein without a fair amount of difficulty—because they don't think about harmony in the same way guitarists do. They're never going to take out a Bach or Chopin piece and see A♭maj7, B diminished and C minor chord symbols above the staff. Harmony is generated by the confluence of individual melody notes. Pioneering guitarist and educator Howard Roberts (founder of the Guitar Institute of Technology) specialized in teaching this approach to harmony, and wrote a column for *Guitar Player* magazine for years that delved into this very subject. Essentially, he would take any common chord and show how it could be manipulated by moving any of its individual tones up or down a fret singly or collectively, yielding dozens of combinations from a single chord form. Play around with this idea for a while and you'll be opening a Pandora's box of possibilities—one that may lead you to new sounds and shaped you've never imagined.

While getting started as a chord melody guitarist, you'll want to keep the above principal in mind, but you shouldn't let it intimidate you. Even the heavyweight champ of solo jazz guitar, Joe Pass, relied primarily on the same tried and true chord voicings reviewed earlier and featured prominently in this book's arrangements. Good voice leading really means that each voice in your chords, when isolated, has a line that can stand on its own, away from its brothers. If you're playing a passage of four-note chords, and you examine what the third voice is doing, and it's jumping all over the place in a jagged, unmusical fashion that's unrelated to the rest of the notes, there's a problem. There should be at least a semblance of continuity there, which doesn't mean that all voices must move the same way, or in similar directions or intervals. The individual line should be strong. Take these examples:

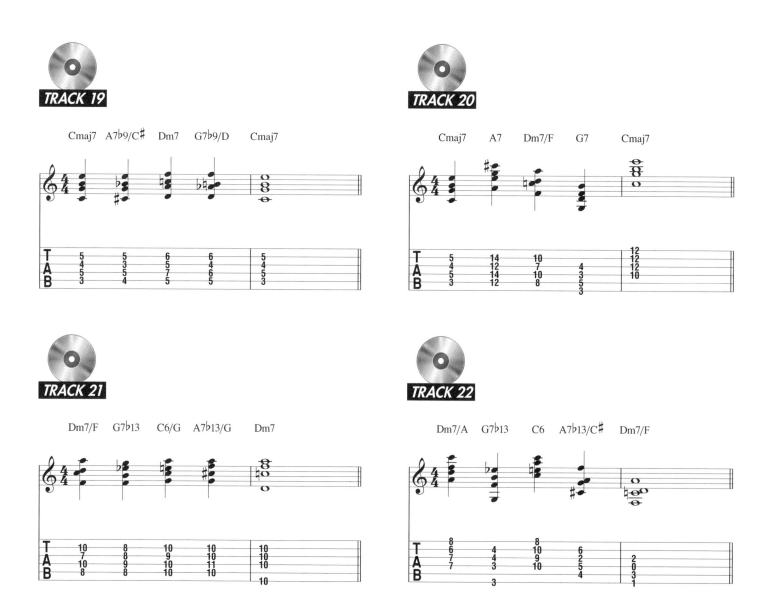

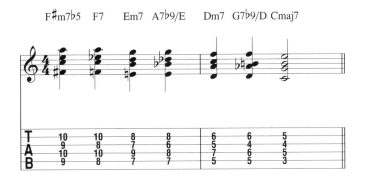

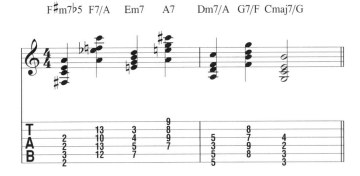

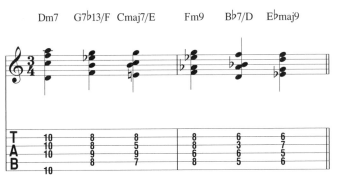

In each example, a common progression is shown first with solid voice leading—each chord tone moves logically and without haphazard motion—then with ridiculous, exaggeratedly bad voice leading. In each progression's second incarnation, chord voices move in outlandish fashion, jumping from register to register with little or no continuity. These exaggerations are shown to make a point—it isn't necessary to have flawless voice leading at all times, but it is essential to avoid disastrous mistakes like these that will have your music sounding bizarre and your hands jumping all over the neck. Examine the voice leading in your original chord melody arrangements, and in your chord playing in a band context, and see if there isn't a way to make things cleaner, simpler, and more musical.

9. Finally, try including shout choruses, interludes and other "send-offs" in your arrangements. They'll help to break up monotony, add excitement, and launch your single-note solos. These can be riffs, pedal points, or other rhythmically propulsive material. Take a look at the second chorus of the arrangement of "Take the 'A' Train," which begins with the riff from the original Billy Strayhorn chart the Duke Ellington band played for many years. How can you hear that and not want to blow a solo? Composed interludes after a "head" (or before it) can change things up as well, providing a break (if simple enough) for the mind and fingers, setting a mood, or allowing you to put your personal stamp on a familiar tune with an original idea.

CHAPTER 5: EIGHT STANDARDS ARRANGED FOR SOLO JAZZ GUITAR

COME FLY WITH ME

Words by Sammy Cahn
Music by James Van Heusen
Arranged by Toby Wine

Let's kick things off with this swinging tune, one of Frank Sinatra's most requested staples. The lyrics paint a picture of youthful and breezy romance and we've tried to stay faithful to that notion and to Francis Albert's interpretation. A rubato introduction gives us a chance to put a bit of our own unique spin on the tune; the chord sequences that alternate with quicksilver single-note runs (a common device in rubato playing) are borrowed directly from the song's progressions. As with other rubato sections in the arrangements that follow, refer to the recording if you're unsure of how these should sound. We fall into a nicely swinging medium tempo in measure 8 for a four-bar extension of the intro before beginning the song proper. "Come Fly with Me" has an unusual form: two 12-bar "A" sections (with different 1st and 2nd endings) are followed by a 16 measure bridge that moves down to the key of the ♭VI (A♭) and briefly to the key of the V (G), before returning to the home key of C. The final "A" section extends to 16 measures and is expanded even further in our arrangement, with a measure of 2/4 that sets up some quarter note triplets aping Frank's cry of "Pack up, let's fly away!" from the original recording.

TRACK 27

MY ROMANCE

Words by Lorenz Hart
Music by Richard Rodgers
Arranged by Toby Wine

Our take on this classic standard is straightforward and swinging. We begin with an introduction based on a common chord sequence that descends from the ♯IVm7♭5 chord (F♯min7♭5) to the IV, iii, ♭III7, ii, and V chords in C. At its end there's a brief G pedal that breaks and allows us to play the pick-up to the song's melody. There are few surprises here, just solid arranging of a well-known and lovely tune that requires little alteration or adornment. Of course, there are some neat little devices thrown in along the way, including the octaves in measure 20, the moving bass parts in measures 24 and 25, a harmonized bebop line in measure 27, and an unusual, James Bond-inspired figure in measure 29. The end of the song is "tagged" with an extension into a III7–VI7–ii–V turnaround and an original melodic theme built on C6/9 and B♭m7(13) chords.

TRACK 28

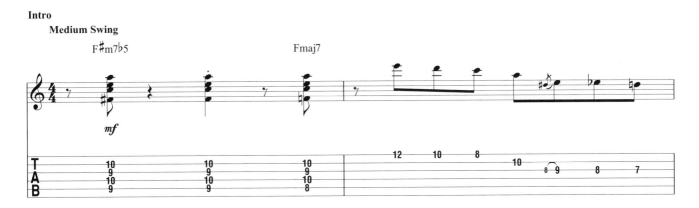

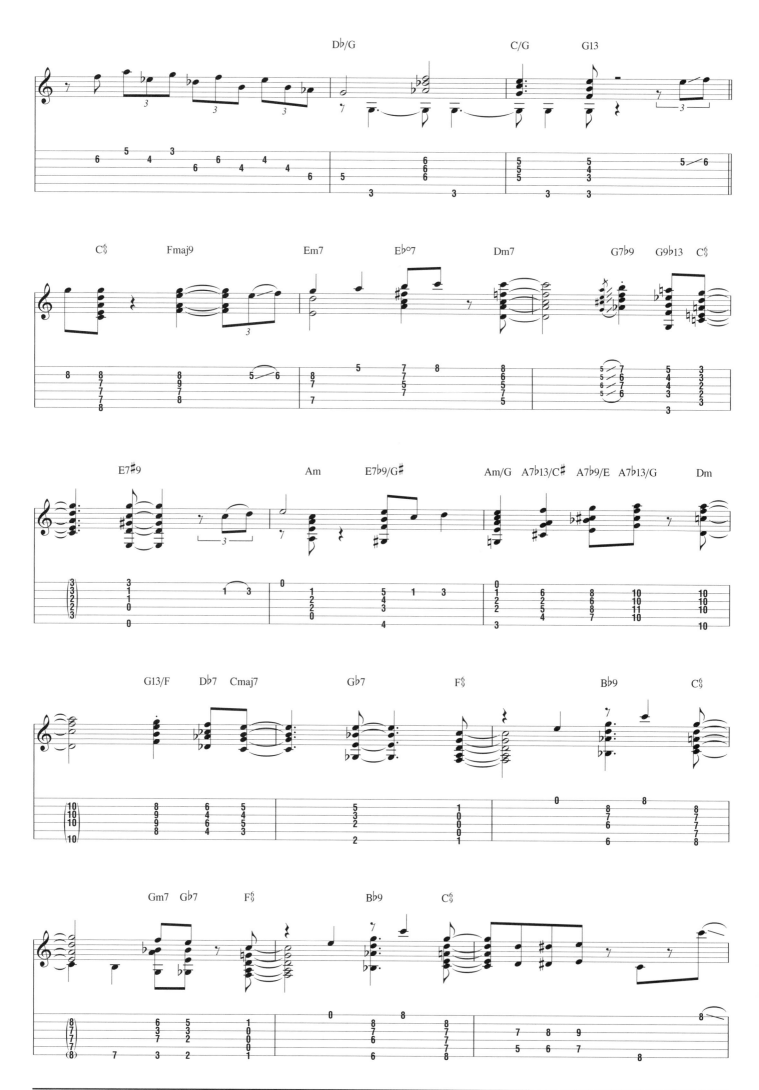

ALFIE

Theme from the Paramount Picture *ALFIE*

Words by Hal David
Music by Burt Bacharach
Arranged by Toby Wine

Burt Bacharach and Hal David's pretty ballad "Alfie" served as the theme song (along with a bluesy Sonny Rollins instrumental) in the film of the same name, a comedy-drama starring Michael Caine set in swinging 1960s London. A four-measure intro (a sequence of ii–V's with chromatic passing chords) at a medium ballad tempo sets up the song. It's unusual to begin a tune rubato after an introduction played a tempo, but it's not unheard of, and that's what we do here, taking our time and pausing for dramatic effect in the first "A," a ten-measure section. The second "A" is played in time and runs eight measures, with a quick run in the final bar. The eight measure bridge features some interesting harmonic activity and an occasional 16th note triplet figure in the bass that's a nod to the somewhat martial rhythms heard in this section in the movie's original soundtrack. We pause again at the end of the bridge for both drama and the chance to whip out a lightning-fast, arpeggiated whole-tone run. The final section of the tune begins by recapping the previous "A" section's theme before turning off into a descending chord sequence, beginning on F♯m7♭5. We return to rubato at the arrangement's end with a series of decelerating passages and fermatas. The original version of the song closes on the second C13sus♭9 chord, but we've tacked on an additional three measures that conclude with our 1st finger playing "C" on the low E string (eighth fret) and our 4th barring the D, G, and B strings lightly above the 12th fret to produce some bell-like harmonics.

TRACK 29

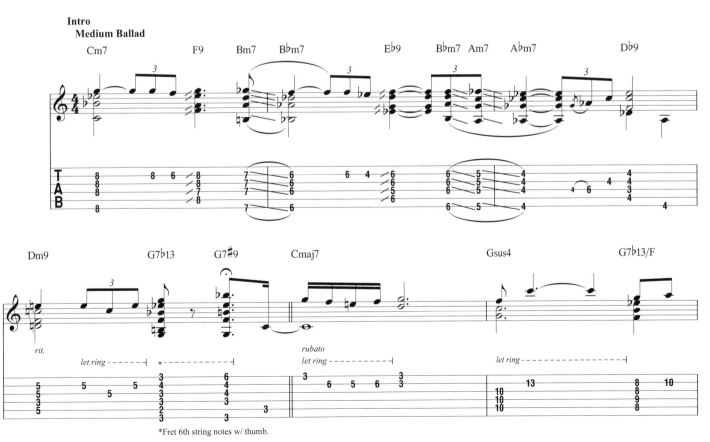

*Fret 6th string notes w/ thumb.

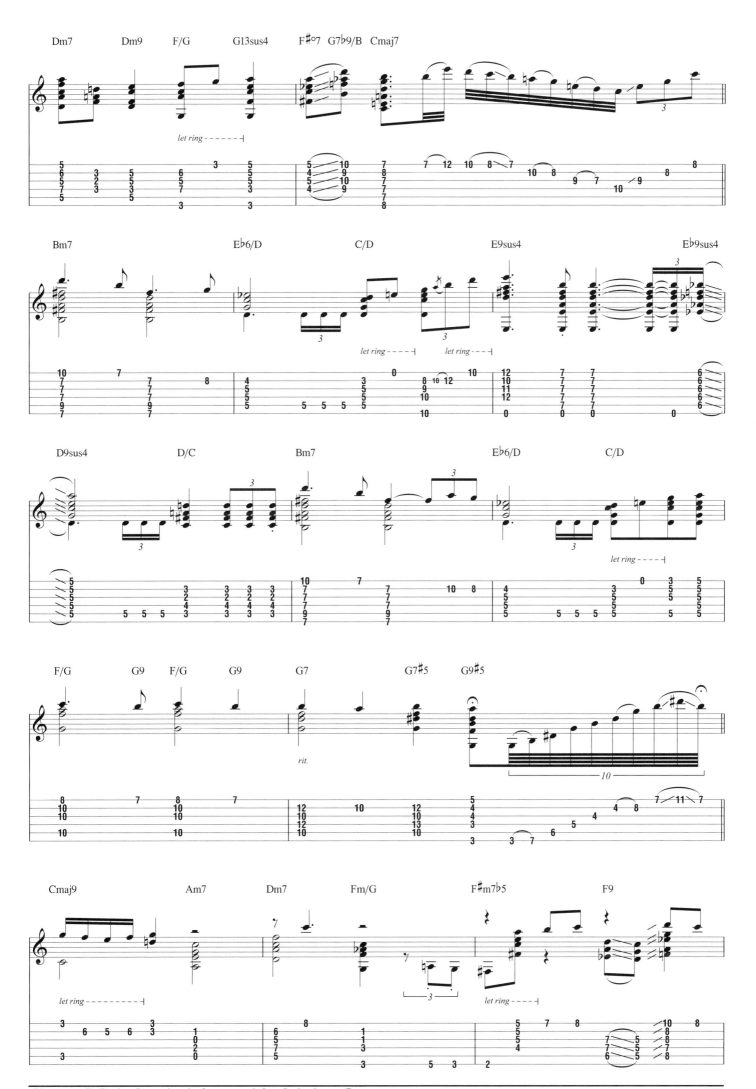

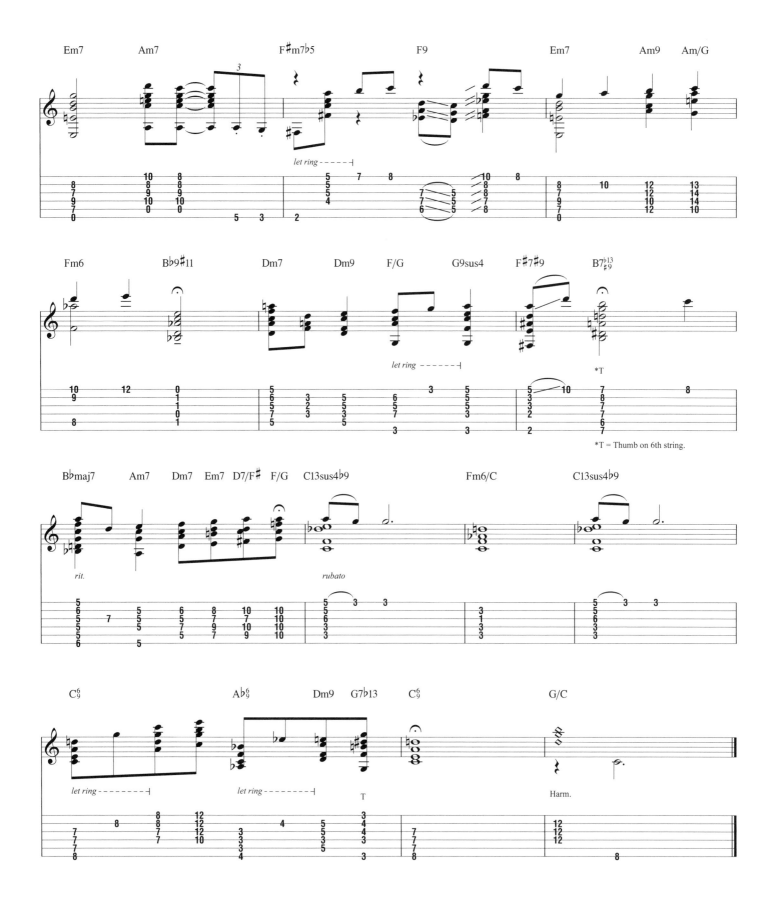

TAKE THE "A" TRAIN

Words and Music by Billy Strayhorn
Arranged by Toby Wine

Billy Strayhorn's "A Train" requires little introduction, as it became the Duke Ellington band's theme song for many years, and one of the most requested standards in the jazz repertoire. Our two-chorus arrangement begins with Ellington's piano intro transcribed for guitar, before breaking into the famous melody. Chords, double-stops, bass lines, and single notes intertwine to create a sense of swinging momentum. The second chorus is set up with a droning G pedal and solo line before alternating between the original "shout choruses" and some bebopish single-note lines. The bridge also illustrates the way we can weave together solos and accompaniment in a solo setting, before returning to the main theme with an unusual reharmonization in the last eight measures.

TRACK 30

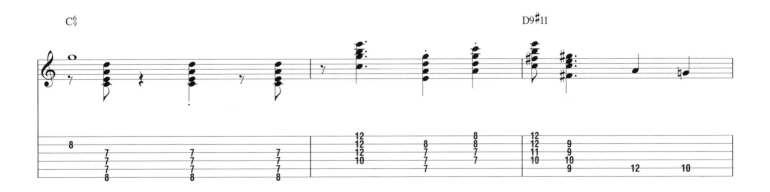

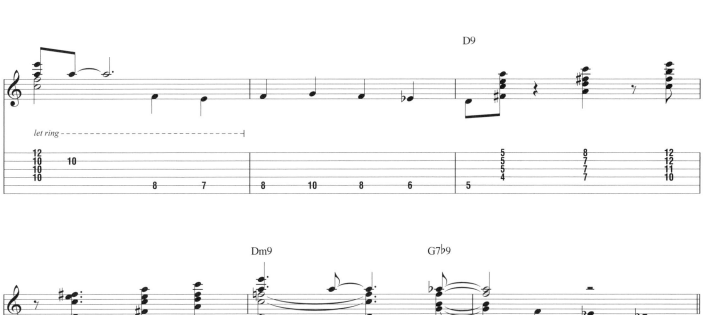

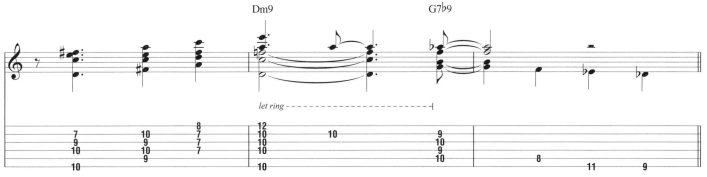

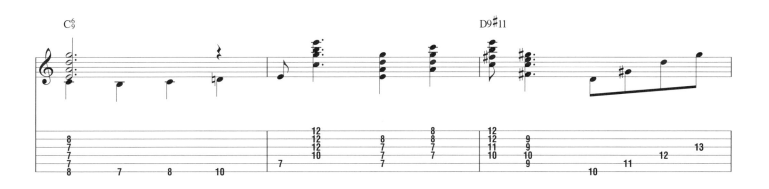

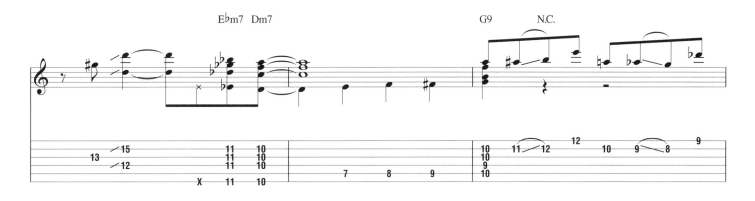

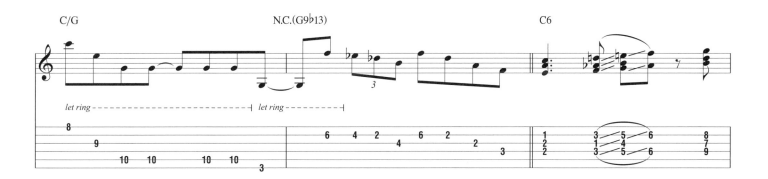

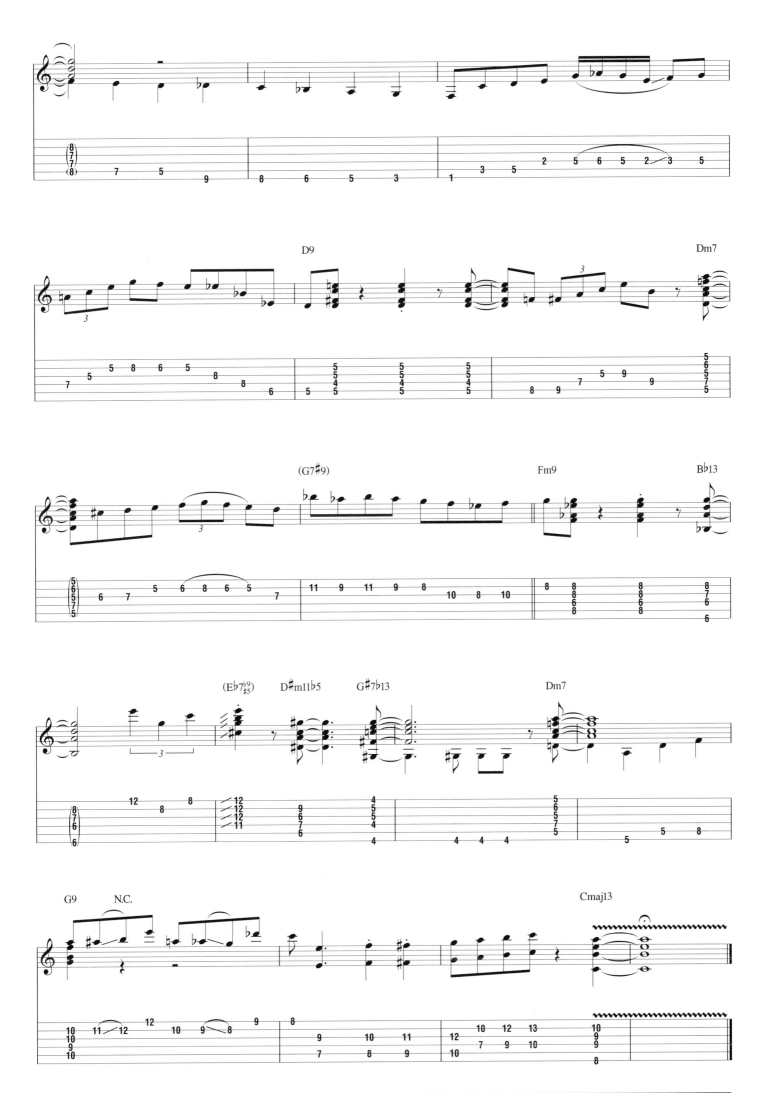

MISTY

Music by Erroll Garner
Arranged by Toby Wine

Pianist Erroll Garner was renowned and imitated for his unique chord style, but he became a real hit maker with his beautiful ballad "Misty," a song every jazz musician worth his salt knows. A very brief ii–V introduction sets us up for a rubato pass through the first eight bar "A" section, chock full of moving bass parts, chromatic passing chords, and cascading single-note runs. We fall smoothly into ballad time for the second eight measures and then end the section with a bluesy single-note line and descending bass movement leading into the bridge. At the end of this relatively straightforward section is a quick, clever series of chromatic ii–V's that moves the whole song up a half-step to E major for the final "A" section, allowing us to use our open low E and A strings to good effect. The arrangement ends with a iii–VI–ii–V tag and a series of descending ii–V's that end on Em9(maj7), our parallel minor. Miles Davis often used this device, ending major keyed tunes on a minor chord, but we relent at the last, giving in to a final Emaj7♭6/9 chord.

TRACK 31

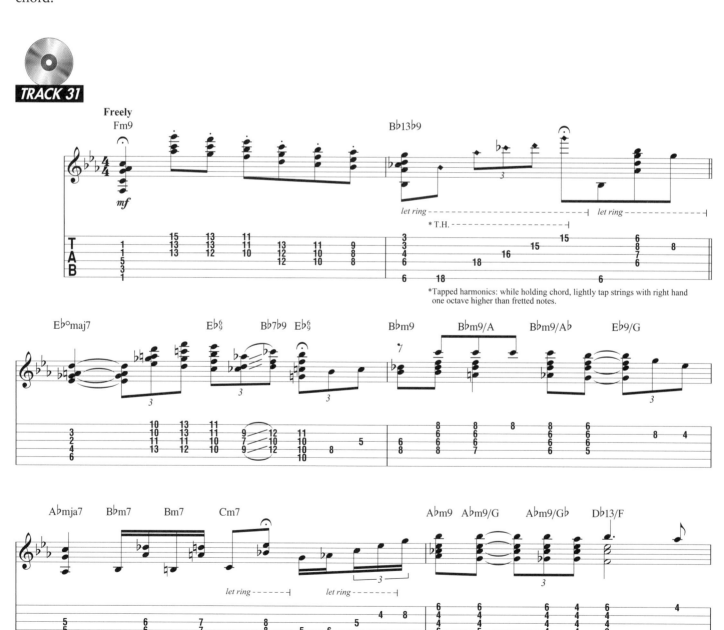

*Tapped harmonics: while holding chord, lightly tap strings with right hand one octave higher than fretted notes.

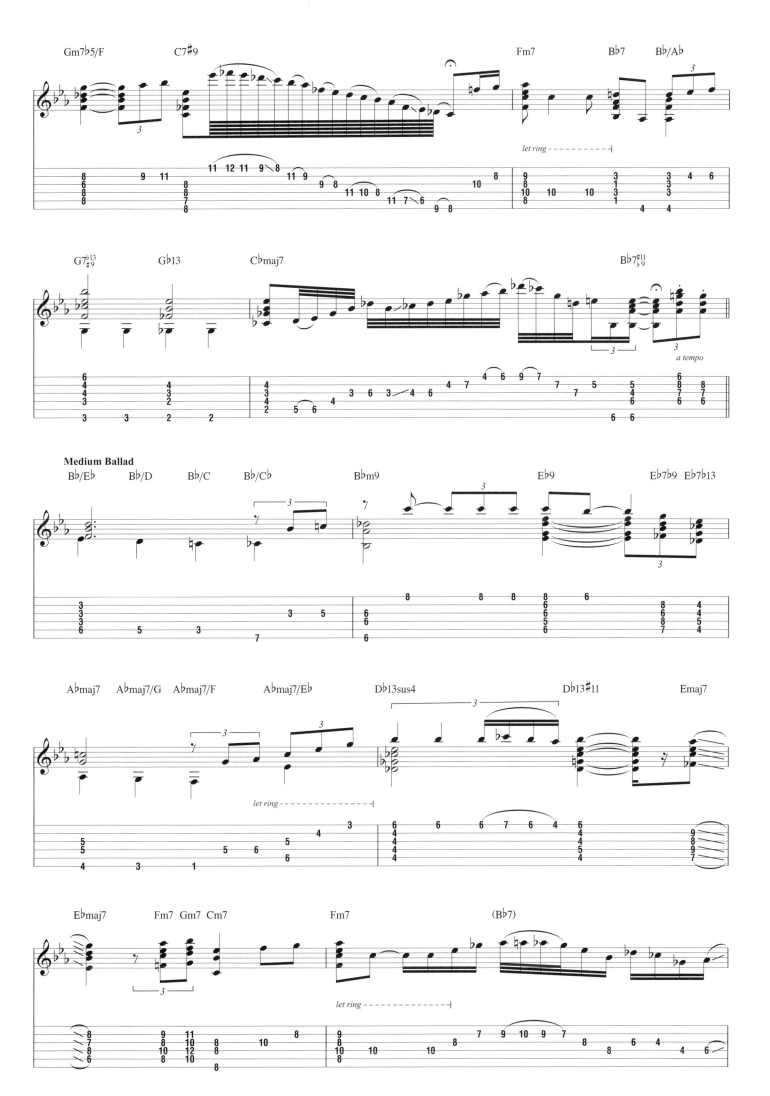

MY FAVORITE THINGS

from *THE SOUND OF MUSIC*

Lyrics by Oscar Hammerstein II
Music by Richard Rodgers
Arranged by Toby Wine

This song was already well known as a Julie Andrews vehicle from the film *The Sound of Music*, but it entered the jazz consciousness as a hypnotic and explosive framework for John Coltrane's soprano sax on his record of the same name, and on subsequent lengthy live explorations. The song is most often played in G major and its relative minor, E minor, so we get a chance to use a lot of open strings here, making our bass chores a bit easier in the process. We begin with some new material—an original 15-measure intro constructed with some exotic chord sounds and pedaling open E and A strings. In measure 16, we break into the little chordal vamp that pianist McCoy Tyner played on Coltrane's studio recording, which is now an integral part of jazz performances of this song. Finally, we begin the pretty, relatively simple melody, played twice in E minor (with 1st and 2nd endings), and then in a transformation that puts us in E major temporarily. The song winds its way back to E minor for its final section, finishes sunnily on a little G to Cadd9 vamp, then returns to the original intro, restoring the darker, ruminative mood we began with.

TRACK 32

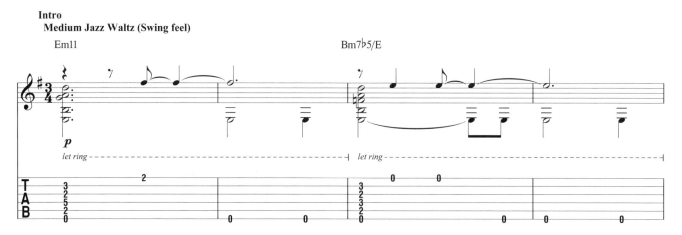

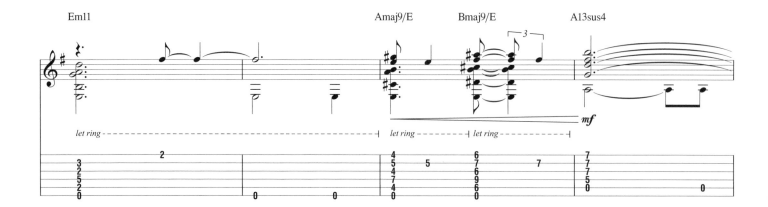

*Strike chord next to bridge.

*Slant first finger of left hand to barre notes at 2nd and 3rd frets.

Chapter 5: Eight Standards Arranged for Solo Jazz Guitar

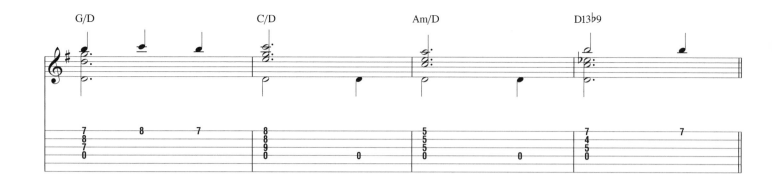

D.C. al Coda

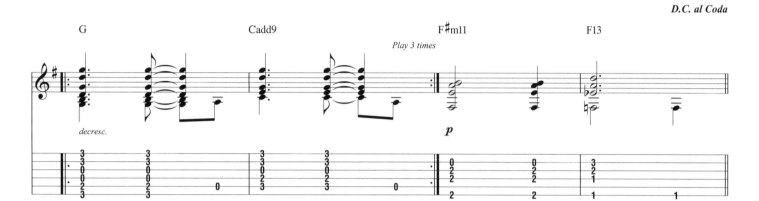

Coda

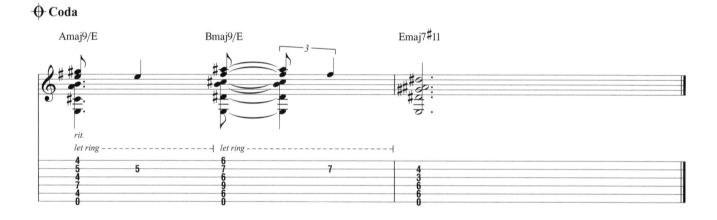

COME RAIN OR COME SHINE

from *ST. LOUIS WOMAN*

Words by Johnny Mercer
Music by Harold Arlen
Arranged by Toby Wine

Another staple of the jazz musician's repertoire, "Come Rain or Come Shine," is given an energetic, quasi-Brazilian treatment here. An eight-bar intro sets things up by vamping back and forth from F6/9 to Gb6/9 and Eb6/9 chords over a latin jazz-styled bassline. We begin with the melody being harmonized by punchy chords, alternating with bass notes—you may find this one easier to play with your fingers than with a pick. The song is stated simply before wending its way back to the vamping groove of the intro. This time, we're in D minor, and we end things by landing on G13sus4 and Db/G chords—the IV (G) of the minor key (Dm)—another frequent jazz practice.

TRACK 33

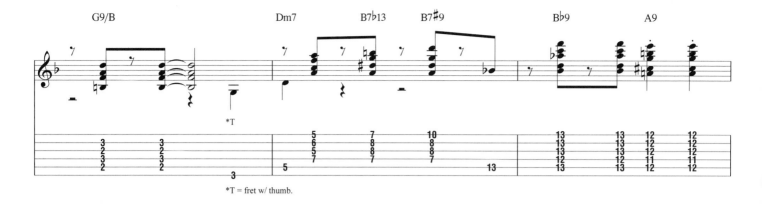

*T = fret w/ thumb.

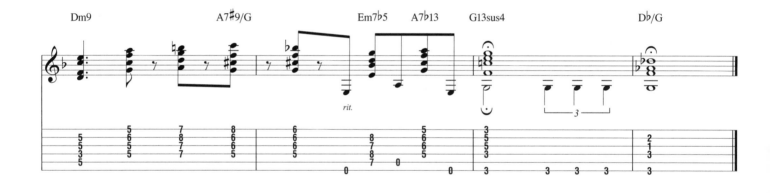

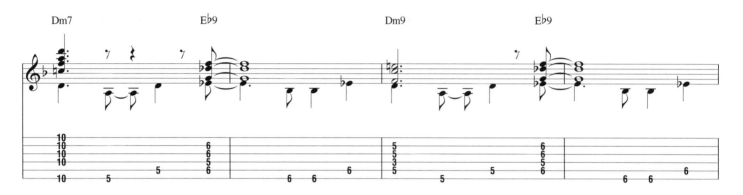

CALL ME IRRESPONSIBLE

from the Paramount Picture *PAPA'S DELICATE CONDITION*

Words by Sammy Cahn
Music by James Van Heusen
Arranged by Toby Wine

Our final arrangement takes an old-fashioned song and dresses it up in some thoroughly modern clothes. An eight-bar intro vamps back and forth between the I (Eb) and bII (E) chords, using shifting voicings constructed from fourth intervals over the open E string. The melody begins at a moderate swing tempo in 4/4. Now, examine the quarter note triplets in measure 16. These will become the new quarter note after a metric modulation in the following measure; the original half note becomes a dotted half note, or full measure of 3/4. The dotted quarter notes in measures 31 and 32 become quarter notes in measure 33 as we return to our original time signature and tempo. The 4/4 to 3/4 transformation occurs two more times in the arrangement, which is otherwise fairly straightforward—4/4 becomes 3/4 again in measure 41, and the waltz feel returns to the original, swinging 4/4 time in the final four measures of the arrangement. These metric shifts are just another tool in the arranger's arsenal, one that can be used to reimagine stale material or place an old tune in a fresh context. This specific kind of metric modulation is not at all uncommon in contemporary jazz—in fact, it's often done on the fly, in an unrehearsed and spontaneous manner, for example, when a soloist plays triplet figures that create a sense of three or six over 4/4. Rhythm section players can respond by adding subtle triplets of their own, or by shifting the time and tempo wholly into 3/4 or 6/8 until a mutual and unstated decision to return to the original time-feel is reached.

TRACK 34

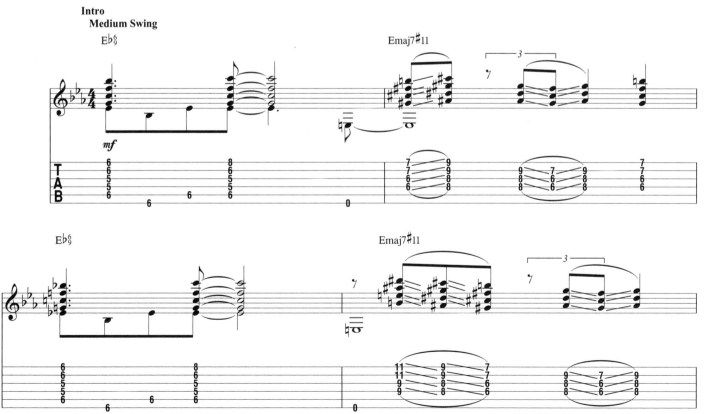

AFTERWORD

By now, you've studied chord forms and inversions, walking bass lines, reharmonization, and other essential aspects of the chord melody style. You've put many of the basic techniques into practice by learning the arrangements in this book. The challenge now is to create your own arrangements of your favorite songs. Ultimately, the experience you acquire may lead to an ability to create these arrangements on the fly in an improvisatory manner, rather than feeling the need to have everything worked out in advance. Great solo guitarists like the late Joe Pass (our patron saint), the legendary Gene Bertoncini, or young lions like Ron Afif, Peter Bernstein, and Russell Malone all possess the unique ability to meld these two approaches, creating new arrangements at a moment's notice or expanding an existing arrangement to include space for soloing and other improvised elements. Jazz is about creativity, self-expression and the need to say new things in new ways. Play sad if you're sad that day. Play frantic if you've had too much coffee. In an ideal world, your chord melody arrangements should be organic and loose enough to allow you to express whatever it is that needs to be said at that very instant. If you play the same tune exactly the same way every time, it will soon lose meaning and immediacy for you and become a rote exercise more than anything else. Be patient with the chord melody learning curve, and keep that jazz spirit!

In closing, I've included a checklist of sorts of things to consider before creating your own solo jazz guitar arrangements. Good luck and keep on swingin'...

1. Begin with a tune you know well. You should be able to sing the melody and play it in any and all keys. Be sure you know how many measures it has and what the form of the tune is (ABA, AABA, ABAB, or what have you). A similar knowledge of the song's harmony will be required as well. Do you know the names of all the chords, their roots and qualities (major, minor, half-diminished, etc.)? It's not enough to know the song is in E♭ and has a B major chord in it. Analyze the tune using Roman numeral analysis and make note of all key changes and other major harmonic movements. If you've worked with singers in the past, these tasks will be nothing new. Accompanists usually have to move songs into odd keys to accommodate a singer's vocal range and often think about tunes in this kind of analytical fashion, i.e. "the tune goes to the key of the IV in the A sections, then moves to the key of the ♭VI in the bridge." This type of harmonic movement will be encountered frequently as one learns more and more songs, and occurs specifically in "Come Fly with Me," which is arranged in this book. The point of all this is that a song is not a chart in a fake book. It's a piece of art composed of at least three elements: melody, harmony and rhythm. Mood, "feel," lyrics, tempo and other facets may come into play as well. To get the most out of a song with your solo arrangement, you'll need to study and honor each of them.

2. Choose a tune (at least at the outset) that isn't super-fast or extremely notey. A Charlie Parker or Bud Powell tune may give you fits if you try to harmonize its quicksilver lines with chords. It can be done, but it takes chops, an extensive knowledge of voicings, and the discretion to know when to harmonize and when to leave a single-note line as is. Any guitarist who's learned his share of "Bird" tunes knows how difficult they are to play in their original, single-line style, and the degree of thought required merely to find the most optimal fretboard position to play them in. Imagine trying to play them harmonized with three or four note chords, or even double stops!

3. Find the best possible key for your arrangement. Just because a lead sheet says B♭, you needn't feel obligated to play the song in that key. Often they'll be shown in the most commonly used key for the song, and as jazz is essentially a horn-player dominated style, they'll be in keys which lay best for saxophonists or trumpet players. These will often be different from the key the song's composer had originally chosen. All these things may be taken into consideration, but don't forget that you're a guitarist and will be playing the arrangement alone, so maximize your instrument's potential. You needn't play everything in E or A—indeed, you should strive for a repertoire that touches as many different keys as possible—but certain chords will sound richer in certain keys, and having the open strings available for drones, pedal points, or lovely, deep bass notes may influence your choice. Take your time and play through the song in several

keys before making your decision. Something that may seem exceedingly difficult or puzzling in one key may reveal itself to be an entirely different animal when shifted a half-step up or a perfect 4th down. Certain keys may leave you in unfavorable registers as well, so you'll want to avoid anything that's too low or way up in the stratosphere of your guitar's fretboard.

4. Consider the lyrics. There'll be no obligation to be faithful to them, and you may find you like playing a tender love song as, say, a frenetic and atonal samba in 7/4. But the words will give you an idea of the song's original "plot" or mood, the essence, perhaps, of what the composer was trying to capture, and may help to put you into a creative frame of mind. You'll be closer to the music and what it was meant to say. You can decide to agree with it, retain its original spirit, or ignore it in the end, but at least you'll know what it was to begin with. Also, specific words and melody notes often coincide in dramatic and meaningful places, something you may want to acknowledge. Many arrangers like to get cute with little musical nods to lines in the lyrics as well, or to pay tribute to famous performances or recordings of a song by quoting or borrowing other ideas from them.

5. Plot the arrangement. Everyone needs to find their own, most effective method of working, but it can be useful to have a blueprint of sorts to guide you. An outline or sketch might include intros, endings, the amount of arranged choruses you'd like to include, interludes, a key change, space for improvised soloing, and the like. You needn't stick to your blueprint, but it can help to keep your arrangement on track and make your work goal-oriented and focused.

6. Work slowly and organically. In contrast to the above approach (or perhaps in addition to it), be loose and spontaneous enough to go where your imagination takes you, even if it veers far off the course you had originally set for yourself. You may wind up walking down musical corridors you hadn't envisioned upon beginning your arrangement. Take your time as well; rather than hurrying through your work to get it out of the way, put it down if you feel it's getting stilted or you're falling back on too many clichés. Sometimes a little distance is enough to supply you with a fresh perspective upon getting back to work. Go onto something else if you're hitting a creative wall, and come back later when the inspiration hits you.

7. Reach for the uncommon. As stated above, it's easy to fall back on clichés, familiar interpretations or the most obvious choices of chord voicing, tempo, or what have you. If an arrangement feels less than thrilling, spruce it up by changing tempo, key, time signature, or mood. Go for that funky, Latin groove or bizarre chord substitution if you hear it and dig it. As a solo guitarist, it's your ball to run with. Take it anywhere your heart desires, even if it is that Sinatra tune everyone else wants to hear the way they remember Frank doing it!

8. Practice the arrangement. Don't sacrifice a cool chordal passage or blistering, pianistic single-note run because they're hard to play. If you heard it, and you dig it, you'll probably be able to learn to execute it at full speed with enough persistence. Switching quickly between unusual and difficult chords may take time and a lot of woodshedding, but your arrangement will be hipper for their inclusion and your chops will be stronger for the work involved.

9. Create an interesting, unique, and balanced repertoire. Include songs in all keys, grooves, moods, and time signatures. Don't be afraid to try new things or to include a pop tune or two if you like them. Maybe you love polkas or merengue or Italian wedding songs—whatever's clever. The jazz scene, like every other music scene on the face of the earth, is populated by staunch traditionalists—the orthodoxy—and convention smashing avant-gardists. Both sides love to tell you (or anyone that's listening) what is and isn't jazz, what's hip and what's "jive" or "square." Try, for your own sake, to tune them out as much as possible. Some of what you hear may be useful, but in the end, you need to stay true to yourself and the unique vision every accomplished musician must strive to reveal. Why else would we toil away in the woodshed for thousands of hours, but for the hope of freeing ourselves from technical limitations and giving ourselves the tools we need to express ourselves fully and without restriction. Remember, even those you admire most are still just human beings with the same subjective opinions we all hold, opinions that ultimately may hold no more or less value than your own.

All forms shown are moveable, thus open strings are omitted entirely. The chord root is circled in each frame.

Seventh Chords and Inversions on the 1st, 2nd, 3rd, and 4th Strings

Fmaj7
(root on top)

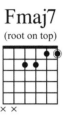

Fmaj7
(3rd on top)

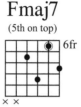

Fmaj7
(5th on top)

Fmaj7
(7th on top)

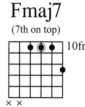

F7
(root on top)

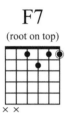

F7
(3rd on top)

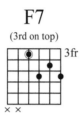

F7
(5th on top)

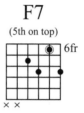

F7
(♭7th on top)

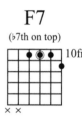

Fm7
(root on top)

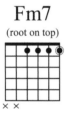

Fm7
(♭3rd on top)

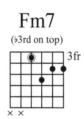

Fm7
(5th on top)

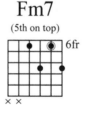

Fm7
(♭7th on top)

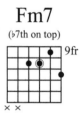

*Fm7♭5
(root on top)

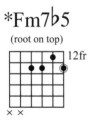

Fm7♭5
(♭3rd on top)

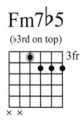

Fm7♭5
(♭5th on top)

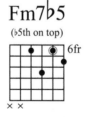

Fm7♭5
(♭7th on top)

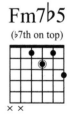

*F°7
(root on top)

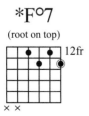

F°7
(♭3rd on top)

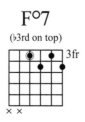

F°7
(♭5th on top)

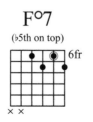

F°7
(♭♭7th on top)

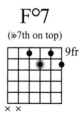

*Chord shown in upper octave to eliminate open string(s).

Seventh Chords and Inversions on the 2nd, 3rd, 4th, and 5th Strings

*Cmaj7
(root on top)

Cmaj7
(3rd on top)

Cmaj7
(5th on top)

Cmaj7
(7th on top)

*C7
(root on top)

C7
(3rd on top)

C7
(5th on top)

C7
(♭7th on top)

*Cm7
(root on top)

Cm7
(♭3rd on top)

Cm7
(5th on top)

Cm7
(♭7th on top)

Cm7♭5
(root on top)

Cm7♭5
(♭3rd on top)

Cm7♭5
(♭5th on top)

Cm7♭5
(♭7th on top)

C°7
(root on top)

C°7
(♭3rd on top)

C°7
(♭5th on top)

C°7
(♭♭7th on top)

Seventh Chords and Inversions on the 2nd, 3rd, 4th, and 6th Strings

Fmaj7
(root on bottom)

Fmaj7
(3rd on bottom)

Fmaj7
(5th on bottom)

Fmaj7
(7th on bottom)

F7
(root on bottom)

F7
(3rd on bottom)

F7
(5th on bottom)

F7
(♭7th on bottom)

Fm7
(root on bottom)

Fm7
(♭3rd on bottom)

Fm7
(5th on bottom)

Fm7
(♭7th on bottom)

*Fm7♭5
(root on bottom)

Fm7♭5
(♭3rd on bottom)

Fm7♭5
(♭5th on bottom)

Fm7♭5
(♭7th on bottom)

*F°7
(root on bottom)

F°7
(♭3rd on bottom)

F°7
(♭5th on bottom)

F°7
(♭7th on bottom)

Seventh Chords and Inversions on the 1st, 2nd, 3rd, and 5th Strings

Cmaj7
(root on bottom)

Cmaj7
(3rd on bottom)

Cmaj7
(5th on bottom)

Cmaj7
(7th on bottom)

C7
(root on bottom)

C7
(3rd on bottom)

C7
(5th on bottom)

C7
(♭7th on bottom)

Cm7
(root on bottom)

Cm7
(♭3rd on bottom)

Cm7
(5th on bottom)

Cm7
(♭7th on bottom)

Cm7♭5
(root on bottom)

Cm7♭5
(♭3rd on bottom)

Cm7♭5
(♭5th on bottom)

Cm7♭5
(♭7th on bottom)

C°7
(root on bottom)

C°7
(♭3rd on bottom)

C°7
(♭5th on bottom)

C°7
(♭♭7th on bottom)

APPENDIX II: MISCELLANEOUS COMMONLY ENCOUNTERED CHORD VOICINGS

Major Chord Variations

Cmaj7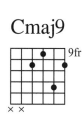
Cmaj9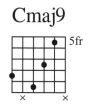
Cmaj9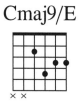
C$_9^6$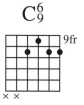
Cmaj7#11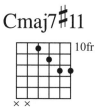

Cmaj7#11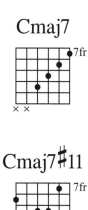
C6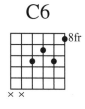
Cmaj9/E
C$_9^6$/E
Cmaj9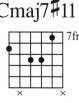

C$_9^6$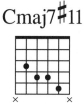
Cmaj7#11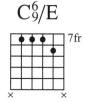
C$_9^6$/E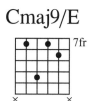
Cmaj9/E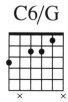
C6/G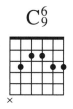

Cmaj9/G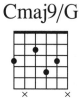
Cmaj7/G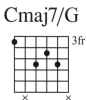

Minor Chord Variations

Cm7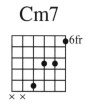
Cm(maj7)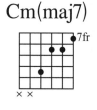
Cm$_9^6$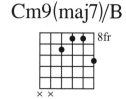
Cm9(maj7)/B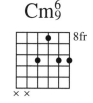
Cm(maj7)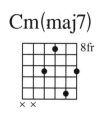

Cm6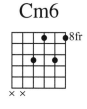
Cm9/E♭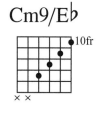
Cm$_9^6$/E♭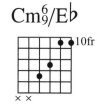
Cm9(maj7)/E♭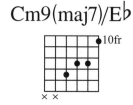
Cm6/A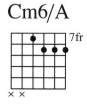

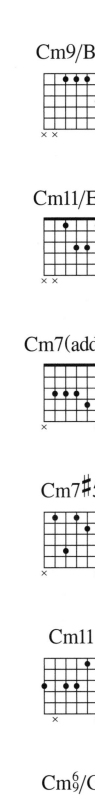
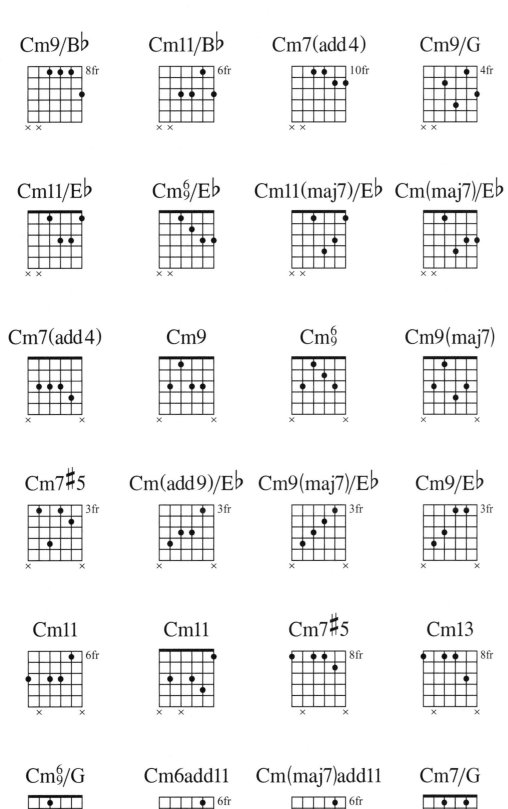
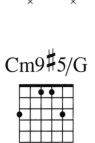

Dominant Seventh Chord Variations

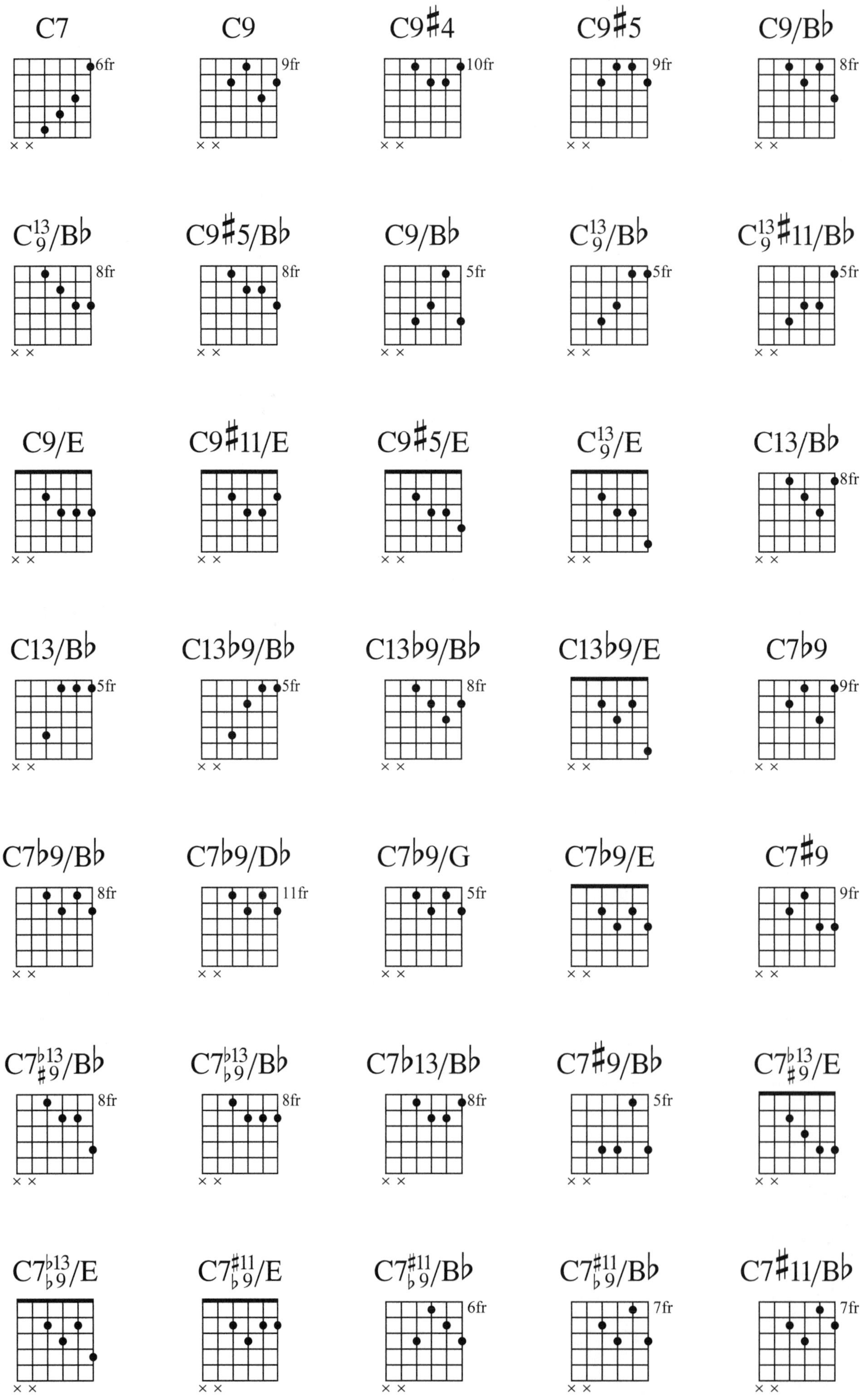
C7
6fr
C9
9fr
C9♯4
10fr
C9♯5
9fr
C9/B♭
8fr
C$^{13}_{9}$/B♭
8fr
C9♯5/B♭
8fr
C9/B♭
5fr
C$^{13}_{9}$/B♭
5fr
C$^{13}_{9}$♯11/B♭
5fr
C9/E
C9♯11/E
C9♯5/E
C$^{13}_{9}$/E
C13/B♭
8fr
C13/B♭
5fr
C13♭9/B♭
5fr
C13♭9/B♭
8fr
C13♭9/E
C7♭9
9fr
C7♭9/B♭
8fr
C7♭9/D♭
11fr
C7♭9/G
5fr
C7♭9/E
C7♯9
9fr
C7$^{\flat 13}_{\sharp 9}$/B♭
8fr
C7$^{\flat 13}_{\flat 9}$/B♭
8fr
C7♭13/B♭
8fr
C7♯9/B♭
5fr
C7$^{\flat 13}_{\sharp 9}$/E
C7$^{\flat 13}_{\flat 9}$/E
C7$^{\sharp 11}_{\flat 9}$/E
C7$^{\sharp 11}_{\flat 9}$/B♭
6fr
C7$^{\sharp 11}_{\flat 9}$/B♭
7fr
C7♯11/B♭
7fr

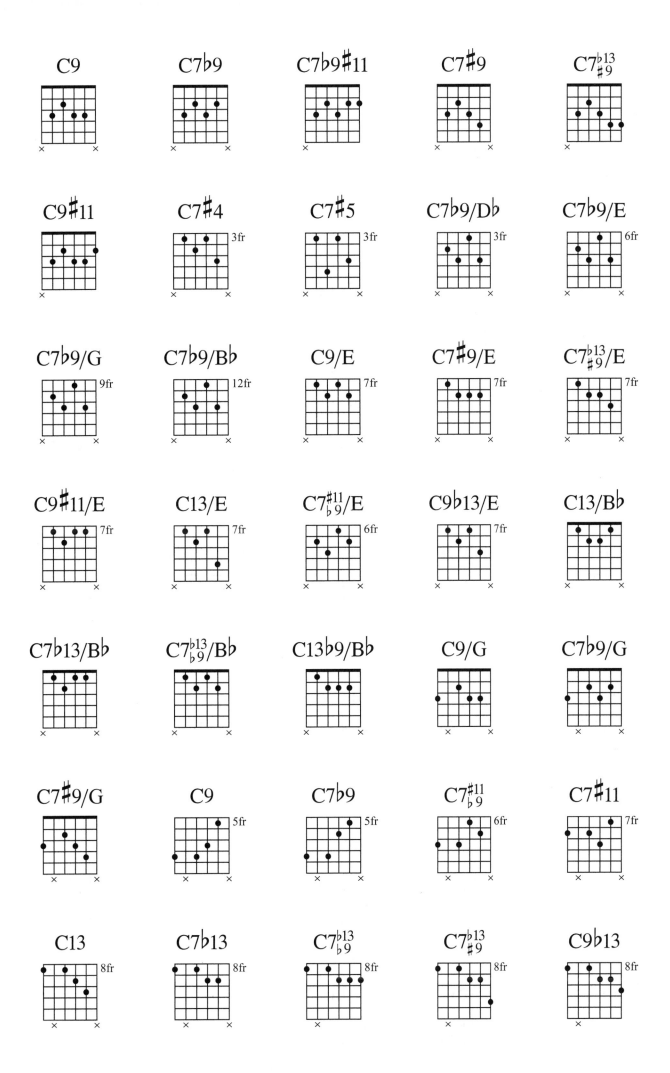

Other Useful Chord Voicings

C°(maj7)

C+7

C7sus4
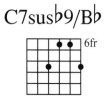

C7sus♭9
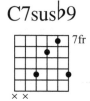

C°add9
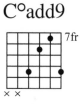

C9sus4/B♭

C7sus♭9/B♭
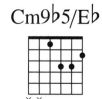

C°(maj7)/G♭

Cm9♭5/E♭

C+7/E
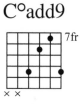

Cm11♭5/G♭

Cm9♭5

C°(maj7)

Cm11♭5

C°(maj7)add11

Cm7♭5

Cm9♭5/E♭

C°7add9/E♭

C°(maj7)

C7sus4

C9sus4

C9sus4

C13sus4

C7sus4/F

C+7

C+7

C+7

C7sus4

C9sus4

C7sus4♭9

C13sus4

C13sus♭9

C°(maj7)